BUILT TO **WIN**

ANNETTE FRANZ

BUILT TO WIN

DESIGNING A **CUSTOMER-CENTRIC**
CULTURE THAT **DRIVES VALUE**
FOR YOUR BUSINESS

Advantage.

Published by Advantage, Charleston, South Carolina.
Member of Advantage Media Group.

ADVANTAGE is a registered trademark, and the Advantage colophon is a trademark of Advantage Media Group, Inc.

Printed in the United States of America.

10 9 8 7 6 5 4 3 2 1

ISBN: 978-1-64225-322-1
LCCN: 2021925692

Cover design by Analisa Smith.
Layout design by Matthew Morse.

This publication is designed to provide accurate and authoritative information in regard to the subject matter covered. It is sold with the understanding that the publisher is not engaged in rendering legal, accounting, or other professional services. If legal advice or other expert assistance is required, the services of a competent professional person should be sought.

Advantage Media Group is proud to be a part of the Tree Neutral® program. Tree Neutral offsets the number of trees consumed in the production and printing of this book by taking proactive steps such as planting trees in direct proportion to the number of trees used to print books. To learn more about Tree Neutral, please visit **www.treeneutral.com**.

Advantage Media Group is a publisher of business, self-improvement, and professional development books and online learning. We help entrepreneurs, business leaders, and professionals share their Stories, Passion, and Knowledge to help others Learn & Grow. Do you have a manuscript or book idea that you would like us to consider for publishing? Please visit **advantagefamily.com**.

ADVANCE PRAISE

I've known Annette for twenty years, and I'm honored to call her a friend. As an advisor to my business, her knowledge and her practical, firsthand guidance on all things customer experience are priceless. This book, grounded in her decades of working with brands to achieve customer and business outcomes, is an invaluable blueprint for a strategy to drive retention and growth in your organization.

—Dickey Singh, cofounder and CEO, Cast.app

Culture. People. Experiences. Profits. Annette gets it—and she shows you how to connect the dots so you can get better results from customer experience and from customer-centric culture at the same time.

—Mike Wittenstein, founder
and managing partner, Storyminers

You can either *talk* about customer culture and customer experience or you can effectively *do* customer culture and customer experience. The challenge is often knowing *what* to do. Annette removes the uncertainty, providing you the steps and the intentions of those steps. Propel yourself, your company, and your program forward in a way that positions you for positive business and people outcomes. This is a must read!!

—Michelle Brigman, former director of CX, 7-Eleven Inc.

Annette brings a refreshing and authentic passion for customer experience to everything she does professionally. She has introduced category-changing thinking while guiding purposeful and adaptable practices with positive results for customers and profitable returns for the companies she works with. Finally, you should know, she doesn't merely keep customer needs in mind—she takes them to heart every single day!

—Donna Peeples, four-time chief customer officer (American International Group, Pypestream, FIS, Envestnet)

I had the pleasure of working with Annette when I was the president of the Gold's Gym Franchisee Association and Annette was with Medallia. The company had purchased the Medallia software in an effort to get all the gyms in the system aligned around the member experience. Annette was my teacher and mentor when it came to how to use member experience data to empower frontlines, align teams, and bring your values and vision to life on a daily basis. It is exhausting to see companies talk about customer experience but never really bring it to life. Annette takes what seems like abstract concepts and breaks them into actionable steps and systems that will help any company put the customer at the center of their universe and win the customer loyalty battle.

—Blair McHaney, president and CEO of MXM; owner, Worx health clubs

PRAISE FOR
ANNETTE'S FIRST BOOK,

*Customer Understanding: Three Ways to Put the "Customer"
in Customer Experience (and at the Heart of Your Business)*

I just wanted to reach out to you and thank you for your truly informative and inspiring book. The thorough explanations on creating customer journey mapping workshops are a valuable resource to me. In fact, the whole book is a valuable resource.

—Joanna Carr, CX consultant, Allegro (via LinkedIn)

I read this great book. Thank you very much, Annette Franz, for it! I strongly recommend you read the book. It describes several principles/processes, which you can reuse in your company. They are really concrete and useful.

—Gregorio Uglioni, head of business excellence and customer experience, Swisscard AECS GmbH (via LinkedIn)

The most actionable book I read in 2019.

—Michael Bartlett, director of experience innovation, JMARK (via LinkedIn)

Annette has been a practitioner in the field pushing that customer rock up the hill. Therefore this resource she has put together is real-world based, practical, and insanely helpful. Read it fully, digest, and reap the benefits. We are all givers with this work—and I applaud

Annette's commitment to getting her great resource out for our community! Bravo!

—**Jeanne Bliss, the godmother of customer experience (via Amazon)**

One time, I pulled out my Kindle in the middle of a business meeting and read aloud from your first book. Really looking forward to the second one!

—**Dave Seaton, vice president of customer experience, nThrive (via LinkedIn)**

When I read this part of the book [the difference between commitment and buy-in], it was a huge "aha" moment for me. Thank you for highlighting the difference. I just gave a presentation, highlighting your book as the inspiration, at the machine learning world conference.

—**Sarah Kalicin, data scientist, Intel (via LinkedIn)**

To the five most important people in my life: my mom and dad, my boys, and the love of my life. You inspire me, motivate me, and fill my heart with so much love—every day.

CONTENTS

Foreword xiii

Acknowledgments xv

About the Author xvii

Introduction 1

CHAPTER 1

What Is Customer-Centricity? 9

CHAPTER 2

Change Is Hard—But You Got This 31

CHAPTER 3

Principle 1—Culture Is the Foundation 51

CHAPTER 4

Principle 2—Leadership Commitment and Alignment Are Critical
to Success. 65

CHAPTER 5

Principle 3—Employees More First. 81

CHAPTER 6

Principle 4—People before Products. 101

CHAPTER 7

Principle 5—People before Profits 111

CHAPTER 8

Principle 6—People before Metrics 125

CHAPTER 9

Principle 7—Customer Understanding 139

CHAPTER 10

Principle 8—Governance

Bridges Organizational Gaps 155

CHAPTER 11

Principle 9—Outside In versus Inside Out 171

CHAPTER 12

Principle 10—Forget the Golden Rule 181

CHAPTER 13

Linking Culture to Outcomes............................. 187

CONCLUSION

A Letter to CEOs 203

Foreword

Annette and I have known each other for many years, having first met in the early days of the Customer Experience Professionals Association at a conference in Atlanta. We connected immediately around a shared interest in customer-centricity as the primary way to be successful in business.

Annette has been at the heart of the development of the customer experience profession for thirty years as a practitioner, consultant, and now globally recognized thought leader, keynote speaker, and executive coach. Her tireless work ethic and commitment to developing approaches that help businesses make customer-centricity a reality are second to none.

It is my great pleasure to share some thoughts on this significant contribution to business leaders everywhere.

Customer-centric culture has long suffered from a lack of understanding as to what it is and the mechanisms that underlie it. Our work at MarketCulture has focused on making this intangible concept more concrete by measuring and benchmarking a company's level of customer culture. (Learn more about MarketCulture's measurement approach in chapter 13.) Annette's work complements our approach and provides leaders with practical tools and techniques to make that culture a reality.

In *Built to Win*, she takes us on a journey through the landscape of what it means to be truly customer-centric.

Annette begins by providing clarity around what the concept of customer-centricity is and how it is different from customer focus—an important distinction, as many business leaders confuse the two concepts.

She then presents four inputs necessary for a customer-centric culture: leadership, core values, employees, and customers, and evolves from there to delve into these topics through her ten foundational principles.

This book provides guidance on the ten principles that must be in place to really bring a customer-centric culture to life. An important theme running through these principles is the foundational importance of the employee experience and how it connects with customer experience. Throughout the book, Annette provides some powerful examples of companies that make this a reality, from Trader Joe's to HubSpot.

While these examples provide us with the inspiration, Annette reminds us it is possible to change and what you need to do to make that happen.

As we say at MarketCulture, a customer culture is to business what breathing is to living.

Enjoy this journey with Annette. You will be better for it!

— **Chris L. Brown**

Coauthor, *The Customer Culture Imperative* (McGraw Hill),
2015 Marketing Book of the Year
Doctoral candidate, Graziadio Business School,
Pepperdine University, Malibu, California
CEO, MarketCulture San Jose, Sydney, Brussels
MarketCulture.com

Acknowledgments

First and foremost, I'd like to thank the team at Advantage|ForbesBooks. When Jacques Wilson first reached out to me in early April 2021 to set up a meeting with Caroline Nuttall to discuss a book concept, I was really waffling about writing my second book with a publisher. I had already planned for the book to be self-published, like my first one. But meeting with Caroline changed my mind, and by the end of April, we had our first draft of the book plan. By the end of May, we had signed our agreement, and I hit the ground running. I had to because I had four months—just 122 days during one of the busiest summers my business has ever had—to get the manuscript back into the hands of the team at Advantage|ForbesBooks. On the eve of that deadline, I'm wrapping up some final edits before I pass the book along to the team to work their magic. I cannot wait to see the final product.

I couldn't have done this without my weekly meetings with Suzanna de Boer, my book coach. You really got me thinking differently about this book. I appreciate your ideas, the examples from and the stories about other authors, the nudges to shift my approach, and just our conversations, in general.

I want to acknowledge those who inspired me, those whose stories I've included in this book, including Bob Chapman, Garry Ridge, Tony Hsieh, Howard Schultz, Hamdi Ulukaya, Patty McCord, and many others. You've taken up the good fight and have truly built winning organizations through caring for your people and creating people-centric cultures that should be the envy of every business leader around the globe.

A huge thank you goes to Chris Brown, cofounder and CEO of MarketCulture, for writing the foreword. We have known each other for many years, and our work aligns nicely. Your guidance, your support, the work you and your father have done, and your vision for a world where customers are at the heart of every business inspires me to continue to push for the same.

Thank you to this huge customer experience profession family that pushes the noodle uphill every day to educate leaders worldwide about the importance of focusing on employees and customers. We've all worked tirelessly over the years to get our message out and heard. And we've often done it together through books, blogs, podcasts, interviews, conferences, book launches, partnerships, and more. You know who you all are, but I'll call out a few here: Michelle Brigman, Dickey Singh, Mike Wittenstein, Jeannie Walters, Dan Gingiss, Adam Toporek, Denise Lee Yohn, Sarah Simon, Jessica Noble, Stacey Nevel, Shep Hyken, Ben Motteram, Jeanne Bliss, Ingrid Lindberg, Jeff Toister, Michael Bartlett, Stephanie Thum, Mary Drumond, Nate Brown, Karyn Furstman, Neal Topf, Donna Peeples, Kerry Bodine, Dave Seaton, and so many, many more. Like I said, you all know who you are.

To you, the reader, I thank you for putting your faith in me and buying/reading this book in order to uncover golden nuggets on how to truly build a winning organization. I walk through life with this purpose: to educate and to help others, in whatever way I can. I hope I've educated and helped you through this book. If I have, feel free to connect with me at AnnetteFranz.com or via LinkedIn or Twitter. I look forward to hearing your feedback and learning how you'll take the principles outlined in this book to heart as you lead in your organization.

About the Author

Annette Franz is founder and chief experience officer of CX Journey Inc. She's a Certified Customer Experience Professional with almost thirty years of experience in both helping companies understand their employees and customers and identifying what drives retention, satisfaction, engagement, and the overall experience—so that, together, you can design a better experience for all constituents.

She started her career at J.D. Power and Associates in 1992 and has since spent the majority of her career running consulting services organizations for CustomerSat, Medallia, Allegiance, Confirmit, and Touchpoint Dashboard—all major customer experience (CX) technology vendors. She's also had three stints working on the client side—at Mattel, Fidelity Investments, and Compellon—in customer experience leadership roles.

In early 2017, Annette left the corporate world to start CX Journey Inc., a customer experience consultancy in which she focuses on coaching and consulting clients soup to nuts on CX strategy. CX Journey Inc. is based in Orange County, CA.

Annette was named one of "The 100 Most Influential Tech Women on Twitter" by Business Insider and is regularly recognized as one of the top thought leaders around the world when it comes to customer experience. She serves as Immediate Past Chair on the board of directors of the Customer Experience Professionals Association, mentors other professionals in this field to help them advance their careers, and is a keynote speaker and an avid writer; you can find her work not only on her own blog but also in *Forbes*, Business2Community, CustomerThink, *Quality Digest*, *APICS* magazine, TechTarget, and more.

She also wrote the book on customer understanding! Annette is the author of *Customer Understanding: Three Ways to Put the "Customer" in* Customer *Experience (and at the Heart of Your Business)*. In this book, she outlines the importance of customer understanding through listening (feedback and data), characterizing (personas), and empathizing (journey maps) to develop a customer-centric culture.

And she is an official member of the Forbes Coaches Council, an invitation-only community for successful business and career coaches. Members are selected based on their depth and diversity of experience. Finally, she is an advisor for several tech start-ups and is an advisory board member for CX@UCI.

Introduction

*Success and profitability are outcomes of focusing
on customers and employees, not objectives.*

—JACK MA

When Dharmesh Shah, founder and chief technology officer of
HubSpot, opened INBOUND 2018,[1] HubSpot's annual customer
event that year, he posed the question, How do you grow better? In
his keynote, he got a bit distracted along the road to answering this
question. But as he meandered through his presentation, he revealed
an epiphany they had early on when his cofounder, Brian Halligan,
who had just attended a CEO networking event, learned that *culture
determines and defines your destiny.*

Shockingly, up to this point, they hadn't spent one second
thinking about the culture of HubSpot—and now they had *this* reve-
lation?! Subsequently, Dharmesh was tasked with defining the culture,
which he struggled with for a variety of reasons, not the least of which
was that he's an introvert and not a people person, and culture is all
about the people.

---

1   Dharmesh Shah, "INBOUND18: 5 Tips from the Customer Code to Grow Better," HubSpot, streamed live
     on September 5, 2018, https://www.youtube.com/watch?v=jC3IxUEyUEA&t=59s

It took some time, but eventually he created a "Culture Code" deck that embodies HubSpot's culture, a deck they still live today, a deck that has been viewed online almost six million times as of midyear 2021.

As Dharmesh continued through his keynote, he revealed that, as a result of all that culture work, his greatest learning about growing a business better was this: *Solve for the customer. Solve for their success. Put the customer first.*

He goes on to say, "In order to grow better, you need a culture that puts the customer first. If you don't have a customer-focused culture, it's not like friction in your flywheel, it's like a full metric ton weight sitting on top of the flywheel. You need to start with a culture where people care about the customer. It makes everything else easier."

It makes everything else easier. To that I say, "Amen." (With one caveat: I will clarify for you the difference between *customer-focused* and *customer-centric* in the next chapter.)

If you've done business with HubSpot, you know that they clearly put the customer at the heart of the business. Need more proof? Dharmesh has also said: "When you're trying to make an important decision, and you're sort of divided on the issue, ask yourself: 'If the customer were here, what would she say?'" That, my friends, is exactly what a customer-centric leader says and what a customer-centric organization does.

Customer-centric companies put the customer at the center of all they do; they ensure that they make no decisions without first thinking of the customer and the impact that decision has on the customer. The customer is infused into everything they do.

I refer to it as putting the "customer" in *customer* experience (CX), which means that companies are taking the time to understand their customers and then using that understanding to design a better experience for them. Too often, companies believe they know what's best for the customer and design an experience based on inside-out thinking, only to end up with customer frustration and dissatisfaction. Why? Because they really haven't put the customer into the experience (design) at all.

> *You need to start with a culture where people care about the customer. It makes everything else easier.*
>
> —DHARMESH SHAH

Customer-centricity can't be solved for with technology. Technology is a tool to facilitate and support putting the customer at the center of the business you are developing and the experience you are delivering. But it is not the most important thing. Customer understanding is; it is the cornerstone of customer-centricity. Once achieved, that understanding must then be socialized and operationalized throughout the organization. It's woven into the fabric of the business.

When you think about companies that are customer-centric or even customer-obsessed, which ones come to mind? Amazon, Zappos, Salesforce, The Ritz-Carlton, Four Seasons, Southwest Airlines, Nordstrom, LEGO, Emirates, and the USAA? Yes, the usual suspects. Wouldn't you like your brand's name associated with those?!

A customer-centric culture is deliberately designed to be this way, and it requires CEO commitment to do just that. It becomes a mindset shift, a behavior shift, and a culture shift.

IS YOUR COMPANY CUSTOMER-CENTRIC?

Why is this important? What are the benefits of designing and living a culture that puts the customer at the heart of the business? First and foremost, without customers, you have no business. So doesn't it make sense to listen to them, to serve them (well), and to create and add value for them? The returns are undeniable.

> **First and foremost, without customers, you have no business.**

According to Deloitte,[2] customer-centric businesses are 60 percent more profitable than their product-focused counterparts. And Aon Hewitt found[3] that a strong culture leads companies to perform higher in revenue growth, operating margin, and total shareholder return.

I'll dive into more benefits in a future chapter, but that sounds pretty compelling to me!

As you think about whether your organization is customer-centric, consider these questions, which I'll address in more detail throughout the book.

1. *What are your company's core values, mission, vision, brand promise, and purpose?* These statements are critical to forming the foundation of your organization. What they say can truly make the difference between a customer culture or not.

---

2   "Customer Centricity: Embedding It into Your Organisation's DNA," Deloitte, accessed November 30, 2021, https://www2.deloitte.com/content/dam/Deloitte/ie/Documents/Strategy/2014_customer_centricity_deloitte_ireland.pdf

3   "2015 Trends in Global Employee Engagement," Aon, accessed November 30, 2021, http://www.aon.com/attachments/human-capital-consulting/2015-Trends-in-Global-Employee-Engagement-Report.pdf

2. *Have these corporate statements been socialized and operationalized?* They cannot remain posters on a wall or, worse yet, hidden on your intranet or website, never to be found—by anyone.

3. *Are your executives committed to and aligned on creating a customer-centric organization?* Executives set the tone for the type of organization you'll have, but first they must be both committed to and aligned on the work that lies ahead to ensure that the business is bringing the customer into all it does.

4. *Are employees and the employee experience a primary focus for your executives?* Without employees, you have no customer experience. Take care of employees, and they will take care of your customers. The employee experience drives the customer experience; it's been proven.

5. *Is the customer ingrained in the organization's DNA?* A customer-centric culture is one in which the customer's needs and perspectives are woven into the fabric of the organization and are, literally, at the center of every decision, conversation, action, process, strategy, etc.

6. *Where do people fall relative to products, profits, and metrics?* Executives must commit to putting people (employees, customers, vendors, partners, etc.) first—before all else. When they put people first, the numbers will come.

7. *Do your executives think they know what's best for the customer, or do they take the time to bring customer voices into key decisions?* Making decisions based on what you think you know about customers is detrimental to the health of the business.

8. *How are employees and customers treated?* Are they treated the way you want to be treated? Or are they treated the way they want to be treated?

I can't wait to hear how you feel about these questions today versus once you're done reading this book.

WHY THIS BOOK? WHY NOW?

I wrote this book mostly for company executives and leaders (including board members—yes, culture must be important to your board!), but it's also for others who want to help executives and leaders understand what being customer-centric means, why it's important, and how to build the business case for building a winning organization where the customer is at the heart of all you do. The point is to help you, the reader, be inspired to act, to think different(ly), and to want to build a customer-centric organization that drives value for all constituents, not the least of which is the business itself.

What equips me to write this book and to drive this conversation? I've been working in this customer experience profession for thirty years. Yes, I started my career in 1992, when I joined J.D. Power and Associates as an associate project director. This was long before the term "customer experience" was even a glimmer in the eye of today's professionals in the field. We spoke of customer satisfaction and loyalty, which evolved to broader conversations over the years to what we now refer to as *customer experience*. Over the last thirty years, I've run consulting services organizations within some of the major customer feedback management platform companies, helping clients in a variety of industries design and execute on their customer experience strategies, and I've had three stints on the client side (at Mattel, Fidelity Investments, and Compellon), doing the same work from the inside. I've seen customer-centric organizations in action. I've consulted on how to create this type of organization. And I've studied others to follow their progress and to see their outcomes and results.

In 2014, the Customer Experience Professionals Association (CXPA) recognized me with a CX Impact Award for work that I had done with a client in the insurance industry. The results were real and impressive. That same year, I also became a Certified Customer Experience Professional, the fifty-second of its kind in the world, earning that certification via a rigorous exam (administered through the CXPA) that provides professional recognition of individuals with high levels of knowledge of the customer experience discipline.

In early 2017, I stepped out of the corporate world to start CX Journey Inc., a customer experience consultancy, and to continue to evolve my work in this field as I learn more about what works and what doesn't for companies across a multitude of industries.

In 2018, I became an official member of Forbes Coaches Council, an invitation-only community for successful business and career coaches. I've also been an advisor for CX@Rutgers, CX@UCI, and various customer-experience-related tech start-ups.

I'm honored to be an internationally recognized customer experience thought leader, coach, and keynote speaker. In 2019, I wrote the book on customer understanding, literally: *Customer Understanding: Three Ways to Put the "Customer" in Customer Experience (and at the Heart of Your Business)*.

CHAPTER 1

What Is Customer-Centricity?

*Customer-centricity should be about delivering value for
customers that will eventually create value for the company.*

—BOB THOMPSON

Customer-centricity is like teenage sex: everyone talks about it,
nobody really knows how to do it, and everyone thinks everyone else
is doing it, so everyone claims they are doing it. In the end, you need
to be a bit daring and just go for it. But first, you need to know what
it means to be customer-centric!

(You've probably seen that quote used for other concepts, such as
big data, digital transformation, artificial intelligence, etc. But it fits
well to describe the state of customer-centricity today too!)

One of my clients needed help putting the customer at the center
of their business. While the leadership team thought they had built
a customer-centric organization, I realized once I started talking to
employees that I was hearing something else. Employees shared with
me that they were struggling with the words and the actions of some
of their colleagues. I probed and found out what I've known for a long
time but which these folks were just discovering in this important
work: *actions truly do speak louder than words.* (I constantly hear "But

we are customer-centric," except people don't really know or appreciate what that means.)

So I asked a group of employees what was happening within the organization. They gave several examples, but one that stood out to me was this: when they asked colleagues in certain departments for assistance with customer issues, they got pushback. The vibe and the responses were "I *am* customer focused in what I'm doing. I'm responsive, and I'm helpful. But I can't help you with your customer issue. Not my problem. Not my job." That's not how winning organizations work. It might be "I can't help you this second," but it's certainly not a hard "No. I can't/won't help you."

The concepts covered in this book are the things that helped to shift the organization back to the center, back to the customer at the center. Specifically, we revisited the core values and core value training, and we established a cross-functional culture committee, which was tasked with ensuring that the culture stayed on track and that employees were living and breathing it day in and day out. We also established an enterprise-wide voice-of-the-customer program and beefed up their employee listening initiatives.

I DO NOT THINK IT MEANS WHAT YOU THINK IT MEANS

There are a lot of articles that refer to a company's "customer-centric people," "customer-centric behavior," "customer-centric tips," "customer-centric marketing," etc. I'm sure you've read many of them. But in the words of Inigo Montoya in *The Princess Bride*, "I do not think it means what you think it means." As the articles carry on, it becomes especially clear that the term that should be used is customer-*focused* behavior. Customer-centric behavior is ingrained in the culture; customer-focused behavior is only for some people (sales, service, and customer-facing employees) or happens at some touch points in the organization. (That's how I view it. They are not two sides of the same coin.) And that's what these articles are referring to: *tactical things* that are being done *in that moment* to ensure that the customer stays, buys, or returns. (Yes, combining those tactical moments across the enterprise can add up to a customer-centric organization, but there's so much more to it than that.)

If you're truly building a customer-centric culture, that means that everyone puts the customer at the center of all they do—whether it's with regard to interactions with the customer in front of you or it's another customer that needs help somewhere else. You don't push off customer issues because "they're not my customer" or "it's not my job" or "it's not my issue." Delivering a great customer experience flows through your DNA. Always.

That dilemma alone drives me to write this book. Helping others to understand what it means to be customer-centric and how to build a customer-centric organization is at the heart of my motivation. Given that, let's look at the two terms in more detail to be really clear on what I'm talking about here.

ARE YOU CUSTOMER-FOCUSED OR CUSTOMER-CENTRIC?

Customer focus means that a brand focuses on the customer. Of course, all brands will say they focus on the customer and may think that they really do. They'll *listen* to the customer (surveys, surveys, surveys), but they don't really take the time to *understand* their customers. And importantly, there's no real differentiation of who customers are—because everyone is actually being treated equally. As a customer. Doesn't that just sound homogenous and lacking impact? They're approaching customers tactically and reactively. It's short term and transactional, and they're only asking these kinds of questions: What does she want? How can we be nice to her? What can we do to get her to buy from us or to come back again? Customer focus happens at the frontline, person to person/face to face. Customer focus is self-serving in that it is used to achieve business goals, not customer goals.

Customer-centric is much deeper than that. In its most basic sense, it means to put the customer at the center of all the business does. (Important point: it does not mean that you will always say yes to everything the customer asks for, nor does it mean that the customer is always right.) And that really means that you take the time to understand your customers and then don't make any decisions without thinking of the customer and the impact that those decisions will have on her. To define a customer-centric organization, I like to say:

No discussions, no decisions, and no designs without bringing in the customer and her voice, without asking how it will impact the customer, how it will make her feel, what problems it will help her to solve, and what value it will create and deliver for her.

It's a way of doing business—a way of being. It's strategic. It's proactive. It's cocreation. It's long term. It's relationships. It's omnichannel. It's enterprise-wide; it's not simply individual heroic efforts. And it's a culture that is deliberately designed to be this way. Customer-centricity flows through the veins of the organization and into everything every employee does—not just if or when a customer is in front of her.

Here's another way of looking at it. Customer-centricity is an approach to doing business in which the business

- focuses on creating a positive experience and delivering value for the customer by understanding the customer, her needs, pain points, problems to solve, and jobs to be done—and by understanding that not all customers are created equal;

- places the customer at the center of its philosophy, operations, and ideas;[4] and
- understands that customers are the only reason they exist.

Sadly, there's a perception gap between businesses that think they put the customer at the heart of all they do and what customers think or believe. In their *The Disconnected Customer* report, Capgemini noted[5] that businesses and customers are "miles apart on the customer experience." They found that 75 percent of businesses believe they are customer-centric, while only 30 percent of customers agree. This is another reason that writing this book is so important. It must be made clear what it means to be customer-centric.

THE FOUR INPUTS OF CUSTOMER-CENTRICITY

To be customer-centric requires four inputs: leadership, core values, employees, and customers. I'll explain each one below and in much more detail as we move through the book.

1. LEADERSHIP

An important thing that I cannot emphasize enough about a customer-centric culture is this: it is deliberately designed to be that way. It doesn't occur by accident. This design comes from the top, from the CEO. The CEO (and the entire executive/leadership team) must be committed to—and aligned on—bringing the customer voice into

---

4   Jake Frankenfield, "Client-Centric," Investopedia, updated April 1, 2021, https://www.investopedia.com/terms/c/client-centric.asp

5   "Customer: What Digital Customer Experience Leaders Teach Us about Reconnecting with Customers," Capgemini, June 28, 2017, https://www.capgemini.com/digital-customer-experience/the-disconnected-customer

all they do. The leadership team must communicate to employees (a lot) what it means to be customer-centric, what their roles are, and how it impacts the work they do. That also means that they must lead by example and model customer-centric behaviors. Leaders are not exempt!

To further perpetuate, they've got to recognize and reinforce behaviors that are in line with customer-centric expectations. Reinforcing the behaviors and actions that you want to see—especially when combined with modeling them—is more powerful than simply talking about them. Remember: *you get what you allow*; what you allow must align with what you've designed.

> *No matter who you are, if you're the boss, the people who work for you will watch you like a hawk for clues about how they should act. It's your responsibility to send the right message.*
>
> —WALLY BOCK

In addition, leaders must always put people first and recognize that their employees' needs come before their own. This should be a basic tenet of any corporate culture: people first, and the numbers will come.

2. CORE VALUES

To further support that the customer-centric culture is deliberately designed, the company's core values must align with and support customer-centricity. Examples of customer-centric values include listening, *wow* (i.e., delight) customers, customer commitment, people first, customers first, deliver *wow* through service, customer obsession, curiosity, obsess about our members, focus on the customer and all else will follow, strong relationships create guests for life, innovation, service excellence, collaboration, customer trust, etc. You get the idea. You don't have to have values that mention the customer, just values that align with the customer-centric culture that you want to create.

And to that last point, it's not enough to just *have* core values; you've also got to *define* the associated behaviors—and then socialize and operationalize them. Go through the exercise of outlining examples of acceptable and unacceptable behaviors relative to each value so that there is no question what they mean or how they translate to customer-centricity.

LINKING VALUES TO BEHAVIORS TO OUTCOMES

A

Description of this value

Behaviors (Acceptable)
Here are 5 or 6 acceptable behaviors that exemplify this value.

Behaviors (Unacceptable)
Here are 5 or 6 unacceptable behaviors for this value.

Outcome(s)
Here are the outcomes for the business as a result of this value.

B

Description of this value

Behaviors (Acceptable)
Here are 5 or 6 acceptable behaviors that exemplify this value.

Behaviors (Unacceptable)
Here are 5 or 6 unacceptable behaviors for this value.

Outcome(s)
Here are the outcomes for the business as a result of this value.

C

Description of this value

Behaviors (Acceptable)
Here are 5 or 6 acceptable behaviors that exemplify this value.

Behaviors (Unacceptable)
Here are 5 or 6 unacceptable behaviors for this value.

Outcome(s)
Here are the outcomes for the business as a result of this value.

D

Description of this value

Behaviors (Acceptable)
Here are 5 or 6 acceptable behaviors that exemplify this value.

Behaviors (Unacceptable)
Here are 5 or 6 unacceptable behaviors for this value.

Outcome(s)
Here are the outcomes for the business as a result of this value.

And don't forget, decisions will be made and policies and processes must be designed with the values in mind so that employees can and will, without pause or question, always do the right thing. Given that, the next step you'll want to take after completing the behaviors exercise above is to identify what the things (rules, policies, procedures, etc.) are that enable or block the correct behaviors.

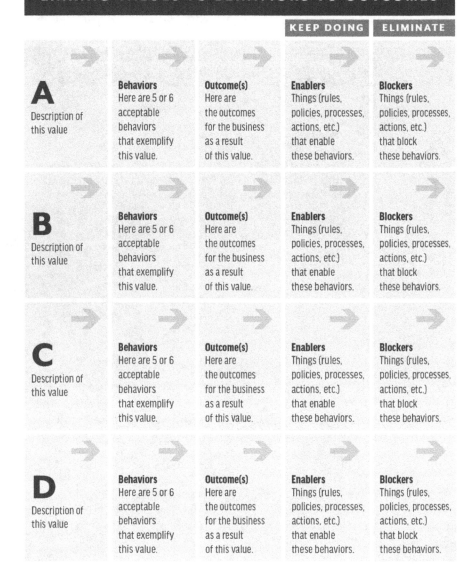

LINKING VALUES TO BEHAVIORS TO OUTCOMES

			KEEP DOING	ELIMINATE
A Description of this value	**Behaviors** Here are 5 or 6 acceptable behaviors that exemplify this value.	**Outcome(s)** Here are the outcomes for the business as a result of this value.	**Enablers** Things (rules, policies, processes, actions, etc.) that enable these behaviors.	**Blockers** Things (rules, policies, processes, actions, etc.) that block these behaviors.
B Description of this value	**Behaviors** Here are 5 or 6 acceptable behaviors that exemplify this value.	**Outcome(s)** Here are the outcomes for the business as a result of this value.	**Enablers** Things (rules, policies, processes, actions, etc.) that enable these behaviors.	**Blockers** Things (rules, policies, processes, actions, etc.) that block these behaviors.
C Description of this value	**Behaviors** Here are 5 or 6 acceptable behaviors that exemplify this value.	**Outcome(s)** Here are the outcomes for the business as a result of this value.	**Enablers** Things (rules, policies, processes, actions, etc.) that enable these behaviors.	**Blockers** Things (rules, policies, processes, actions, etc.) that block these behaviors.
D Description of this value	**Behaviors** Here are 5 or 6 acceptable behaviors that exemplify this value.	**Outcome(s)** Here are the outcomes for the business as a result of this value.	**Enablers** Things (rules, policies, processes, actions, etc.) that enable these behaviors.	**Blockers** Things (rules, policies, processes, actions, etc.) that block these behaviors.

3. EMPLOYEES

A customer-centric culture puts employees more first because it cannot exist unless the employees "live it." (Well, there is a culture, but it's not the one you want or have designed for.) Values are meaningless unless they inspire and drive the behavior that you expect your employees and executives to display. In other words, your core values will only mean something if everyone in the company knows what they mean and actually lives them.

Once you've established the behaviors related to each core value, you've got to ensure that employees have the proper training, tools, and resources to live and breathe them. And they must be empowered to do what you expect them to do. Empowering employees is a sign that you trust them. For example, The Ritz-Carlton is well known for its $2,000 rule, which gives every employee the ability to spend up to $2,000 per guest per incident should there be an issue. No management approval or input is required. For customers, it's such an unexpected action on the part of the hotel that it not only creates word of mouth that goes viral but also builds trust and drives loyalty. Who wouldn't want to continue to do business with a brand that shows it cares by going the extra mile when needed?

It might surprise you to hear, too, that hiring for *culture fit* is important to getting the customer-centric culture you want. You've got to get the right people on the bus, the people—leaders and individual contributors alike—whose values and purposes align with your company's value and purpose. Hire for attitude; train for skill. When you hire

> When you hire people who **really** care about people, a customer-centric culture is much easier to create.

17

people who *really care* about people, a customer-centric culture is much easier to create. (On that note, do you actually mention customers and the customer experience in your job descriptions and postings? Why wouldn't you? When people know their work is linked to customers and to customer outcomes, it creates a powerful connection. And you get employees in those roles that truly are "people people.") And when you have a culture where people care about people, your employer brand attracts—and makes finding—the right talent much easier.

4. CUSTOMERS

Customer understanding is the cornerstone of customer-centricity. You can't have a customer-centric culture without customers, without bringing the customer voice into the business—and then, of course, doing something with it! A customer-centric business is informed by customers, and its purpose (the purpose of every business, really) is to create and to nurture those customers.

You've got to use the data and the insights gained during your customer understanding work to design and deliver an experience that solves customer problems, helps them achieve the jobs they are trying to do, and addresses their pain points. In short, you've got to deliver value to your customers in order to achieve business value. This is the heart and the spirit of customer-centricity.

Your culture is a combination of what you create and what you allow.

—CRAIG GROESCHEL

Being customer-centric happens by design. Customer-centric companies do the following to ensure the organization knows its reason for being (i.e., the customer) and to embed the customer into the DNA of the organization. Use the column on the right to indicate how many of these you have or do in your organization. You can also find this assessment at AnnetteFranz.com.

CUSTOMER-CENTRIC COMPANIES ...	IN MY COMPANY ...		
	We Do This	We Sorta Do This	We Don't Do This
Have visible (and visibly) customer-centric leadership, demonstrating a customer commitment from the top down	☐	☐	☐
Have a C-suite executive (e.g., a chief customer officer, CCO) who champions the customer across the entire organization	☐	☐	☐
Have a customer experience vision that aligns with the corporate vision (or they are one and the same)	☐	☐	☐
Develop and socialize customer personas	☐	☐	☐
Speak and think in the customer's language	☐	☐	☐
Use customer feedback and data to better understand their customers	☐	☐	☐
Are engaged in continuous improvement as a result of the customer understanding efforts	☐	☐	☐
Focus on products and services that deliver value for their customers (i.e., solving their problems and helping them with the jobs to be done)	☐	☐	☐
Have a commitment to customer success	☐	☐	☐
Engage with customers from the beginning	☐	☐	☐
Walk in the customer's shoes to understand today's experience in order to design a better experience for tomorrow	☐	☐	☐
Empower the frontline to do what's right for the customer	☐	☐	☐

CUSTOMER-CENTRIC COMPANIES ...	IN MY COMPANY ...		
	We Do This	We Sorta Do This	We Don't Do This
Recognize the customer across all channels	☐	☐	☐
Design processes and policies from the customer's point of view	☐	☐	☐
Measure what matters to customers	☐	☐	☐
Keep an eye on the competition but don't make the competition the focal point	☐	☐	☐
Use cocreation and customer-led innovation—in other words, innovation starts with the customer	☐	☐	☐
Include customer-driven values in their core values	☐	☐	☐
Recruit and hire employees passionate about customers and about helping customers	☐	☐	☐
Incorporate the customer and the customer experience into their onboarding processes	☐	☐	☐
Train employees on how to deliver the experience that customers expect	☐	☐	☐
Establish a customer room that is open to employees 24-7 so that they can learn more about their customers and the customer experience	☐	☐	☐
Use rewards and recognition to reinforce employee behaviors that align with customer-centricity	☐	☐	☐
Put customers before metrics (e.g., every meeting begins with and includes customer stories)	☐	☐	☐
Invest in the latest technology to support, facilitate, and deliver the experience customers expect—but know that the experience is very much human	☐	☐	☐

As you can see, becoming a customer-centric organization is a commitment that requires a mindset shift and a behavior shift, which I'll explain in the next chapter, and especially, some investments—financial, human, time, resources, technology, and more.

TEN KEY PRINCIPLES

While the above are four critical *inputs* to a customer-centric organization, there are also 10 key *defining foundational principles* built upon those inputs that ensure that customer-centricity is an enterprise-wide approach to doing business. These principles are the framework upon which this book is based and the framework upon which your winning organization must be built.

1. Culture is the foundation.
2. Leadership commitment and alignment are critical to success.
3. Employee experience: employees must be put more first.
4. People come before products.
5. People come before profits.
6. People come before metrics.
7. Customer understanding is the cornerstone.
8. Governance bridges organizational gaps.
9. Outside-in thinking and doing versus inside-out thinking and doing are core.
10. The Platinum Rule[6] rules.

---

6   The Platinum Rule is a registered trademark of Dr. Tony J. Alessandra.

WHY CUSTOMER-CENTRICITY?
IT'S ABOUT THE BENEFITS.

Customer-centric organizations are winning organizations. If you put forth the effort to align with these ten principles, you will reap the *benefits*. I already mentioned in the introduction that profitability is a benefit, but there's more! And benefits are attributed to both humans (employees and customers) and to the business. Let's start with the human side.

Fix the culture, fix the outcomes.

When the business is customer-centric, customers feel it. (Just think about your own interactions with the "usual suspect" brands that I mentioned earlier.) Customers know they matter to the business. They know you listen; they see how you solve problems and deliver value. When you deliver value for customers, you also create value for the business. When this happens—when customers know you listen and, in turn, deliver value—you are on the road to building longer-term relationships with them.

Putting customers at the center of all you do means
that customers are a little more forgiving too.

But customer-centricity isn't just about customers; it's about your employees too. Without employees, you have no customer experience! In order to have happy, loyal customers, you have to care for your employees and treat them well. At the end of the day, your business focus has to be on the people who drive your business—both employees and customers (and vendors, partners, etc.). There can be no customer-centric culture without focusing on your employees more first. Employees reap the benefits, for sure!

By definition, a customer-centric culture is a collaborative culture. By definition, the entire organization rallies around the customer. Also by definition, the entire organization must work toward a common goal to deliver a seamless and consistent experience for the customer. That cannot happen in a fragmented organization. It can only happen when everyone works together. That is a major benefit for customers and for employees. Breaking down or connecting silos takes some of the effort out of the experience for both employees and customers.

And that also contributes to this next benefit, consistency. Customer-centric businesses also value consistency and delivering consistently. Customers always know what to expect from customer-centric businesses because they have heard the brand promise and have experienced it. For example, Trader Joe's (a leading food retailer that is extremely successful in their market) brand promise is "We just focus on what matters: great food + great prices = Value." No smoke and mirrors. I love shopping there, as do so many others. Why? Expectation set and promise delivered on consistently, every time. You know what you're going to get every time you shop at Trader Joe's. That consistency also builds trust, which is a solid foundation for any relationship.

Innovation is another benefit of customer-centric businesses. This benefit bridges the business and the human sides of this story. Customers provide feedback. Businesses listen, cocreate, and innovate to solve customer problems. Customers *and* the business win.

On the business side of the story, the benefits of customer-centricity are numerous. A good segue from innovation is growth; when

Who wouldn't want to work for— or buy from— a company that cares about people?

23

you innovate to solve for unfulfilled needs and other problems, you are bound to attract potential/future customers who didn't even know they had these problems to solve—or for whom these problems appear at a later time. New problems solved = new customers = growth.

Customer-centricity provides a competitive advantage for the business, too, both from an employee as well as a customer perspective. Who wouldn't want to work for—or buy from—a company that cares about people? Again, think about your own experiences with the brand examples I provided earlier. If you don't know anyone who works for these brands, head over to Glassdoor or to Great Place to Work and read there what employees are saying.

Other benefits for the business include the following:

- **Increased retention and customer lifetime value:** customers want to continue to do business with brands that listen to them, care about them, solve their problems, and create value for them.
- **Increased loyalty:** not only do customers stay, but they buy more, spend more, etc.; customer-centric organizations focus on journeys, not just on touch points, which means that they focus on relationships, not transactions.
- **Increased referrals:** all of that customer love leads to a supplemental marketing and sales force (your customers!) that can't wait to advocate for your brand.
- **Reduced costs:** when brands listen to customers and use that feedback to make improvements, they realize operational efficiencies through process improvements and more.
- **Increased revenue:** it's easier to sell products when they solve problems for your customers, and they solve problems because you took the time to understand customers.

THE LINK BETWEEN CULTURE AND BUSINESS SUCCESS OR FAILURE

Need more proof that customer-centric organizations are winning organizations? Duke University's Fuqua School of Business did some research a couple of years ago. The findings are quite interesting, as they uncovered the link between culture and both business successes and business failures.

One of their research papers, *Corporate Culture: The Interview Evidence,*[7] is based on surveys of both 1,348 CEOs and chief financial officers (CFOs) and in-depth interviews with executives representing 20 percent of the US equity market capitalization. Questions addressed in this paper included the following:

1. What is corporate culture?
2. How important is corporate culture?
3. What mechanisms underlie the creation and effectiveness of corporate culture? How do other formal institutions (e.g., governance or compensation) reinforce or work against culture?
4. Do companies think their culture is effective, and if not, what deters firms from having an effective corporate culture?
5. Are the upside benefits of an effective culture greater than the downside costs of ineffective culture?
6. What aspects of business performance does corporate culture affect? Does culture impact firm value, productivity, corporate risk-taking, growth, mergers and acquisitions (M&A), financial and tax reporting, whether employees take a long-run view, and/or corporate ethics?
7. How can corporate culture be measured?

---

7   "Corporate Culture: The Interview Evidence," Duke University, accessed November 30, 2021, https://papers.ssrn.com/sol3/papers.cfm?abstract_id=28428

The answers to these questions are fascinating and really support everything we (certainly, I) tend to believe and write/talk about when it comes to corporate culture and how critical it is to a business.

Some interesting findings from this research include the following:

- Most executives would walk away from an M&A deal if the target acquisition is not aligned culturally with their existing cultures; others would require a heavy discount on the purchase price.
- Culture is set by the CEO.
- The board doesn't drive culture but can influence it through their choice of a CEO.
- Executives agree that for a culture to be effective, the values must be backed up by behaviors and norms.
- Culture is a top-three value driver of the business and one of the most important forces behind value creation.
- An effective culture improves the company's value and profitability through the following:
  - fostering creativity and encouraging productivity,
  - higher risk tolerance,
  - mitigating myopic behavior, and
  - creativity and innovation.

- Effective cultures (a culture that promotes employee behaviors that drive successful execution of the company's strategies) happen when the company walks the talk and lives the values.
- An ineffective culture (one that does not promote those behaviors and might even work against the right behaviors) increases the chances that employees will act unethically or illegally.
- Few executives agreed that their culture is where it ought to be.

- Why not? Leadership needs to invest more time to develop the culture.

- Ways to measure the existing culture include the following:
  - conference call transcripts/analyst calls;
  - employee age, tenure, and turnover;
  - external communications by the company;
  - portrayal of the CEO in the press;
  - understanding the circumstances around a CEO change;
  - employee opinions (e.g., on Glassdoor);
  - assessments of whether the culture is aligned with the needs of the business;
  - evaluation of internal communication patterns; and
  - management actions.

These are just some of the highlights from this research. There is so much great information in this report; I recommend taking the time to download it at AnnetteFranz.com. I don't think you'll be disappointed by what you will learn!

In the aforementioned Capgemini report, *The Disconnected Customer*, they compared customer-centric leaders and laggards and found a sixty-nine-point gap in Net Promoter Score (NPS) between the two, with leaders seeing a thirteen-point increase over the last three years and laggards only seeing a two-point increase. They also found that leaders saw a 41 percent decrease in spending, on average, due to a bad customer experience, while laggards saw a 53 percent decrease. What do those numbers tell you? The answer is clear. Putting customers at the center of all you do means that customers are a little more forgiving too.

One more data point: in KPMG's "2018 Global Consumer Executive Top of Mind Survey,"[8] KPMG found that companies that put the customer at the heart of their businesses enjoy higher revenue growth, profit growth, and customer scores than those who don't.

If there's any doubt in your mind that customer-centricity is good for employees, good for customers, and good for the business, those benefits and statistics should clear that up.

Change is inevitable. Growth is optional.

—JOHN C. MAXWELL

But here's the thing: becoming a winning organization built on a foundation of customer-centricity doesn't just happen by chance or on its own. It requires you to do things differently. It requires a change—and it begins with you. It begins with you leading the organization through a transformation that might seem daunting but necessary. Change is scary, but winning is not.

Take a minute to do this quick assessment, and then let's dive into the next chapter to identify what's holding you back and how you can push through that to build the business you know you want!

IS YOUR ORGANIZATION CUSTOMER-CENTRIC?

Now that you know what a customer-centric organization looks like, let's do a quick assessment of yours.

---

8   "2018 Top of Mind Survey," KPMG, accessed November 30, 2021, https://home.kpmg/ua/en/home/insights/2018/07/top-of-mind-survey-2018.html

DO YOU SEE ...	WHAT TO DO?	OUTCOMES OR BENEFITS
Singular hero employees doing what's right for customers?	Empower all employees to be heroes; don't just expect your front line or your "people persons" to be the heroes.	Consistent positive experience across all channels for the customer.
Leaders or employees who don't live the core values?	Have a conversation to find out why. What's holding them back?	Getting everyone on board with the desired culture, getting the culture you designed for.
Leaders or employees who don't understand the importance of a great customer experience and a customer-centric culture?	Provide a clear line of sight to ensure that leaders and employees understand every aspect of how their performances are important to the customer's best possible outcome.	A better employee experience and customer experience.

CHAPTER 2

Change Is Hard—But You Got This

All great changes are preceded by chaos.

—DEEPAK CHOPRA

Deepak Chopra's quote hit me hard. It rings loud and true as we leave 2020 in the rearview mirror. We have seen that, through uncertainty and uncharted times—and even chaos—when change is needed, it can and will and does happen. We can innovate if we need to. We can repurpose if we need to. We can be nimble. We can do things differently if we need to. We can band together for a common cause or purpose. We can change if we need to.

While that's a lot of "if we need to," the point is that you *know* your organization needs to change. Deep down inside you know. You knew then, and you know now. It's time to do things different(ly).

I'm calling bullshit on the "change is not easy in our company" or the "we can't change" excuses going forward. If companies can pivot and manufacture completely different products or can move their entire workforces from their offices to their homes in a matter of days (during the pandemic), then perhaps it's not that hard. We learned a lot about ourselves in 2020—as individuals, as leaders, and as businesses. The important thing is to take those learnings and view them as opportunities to do things differently going forward.

Arundhati Roy noted in her *Financial Times* article[9] in April 2020 an interesting perspective about difficult times being a portal for change: "Historically, pandemics have forced humans to break with the past and imagine their world anew. This one is no different. It is a portal, a gateway between one world and the next … We can walk through lightly, with little luggage, ready to imagine another world. And ready to fight for it."

You must use the opportunities presented to you as portals to the future state, to the next normal.

She also noted: "And in the midst of this terrible despair, it offers us a chance to rethink the doomsday machine we have built for ourselves. Nothing could be worse than a return to normality."

Nothing could be worse than a return to normality.

—ARUNDHATI ROY

While I'm not comparing organizational change to what happened in India or in the rest of the world, nor am I stating that you've built a doomsday machine instead of a viable, thriving brand, the words are important and relevant. During the pandemic, you were exposed to your business's greatest pains, vulnerabilities, and performance improvement opportunities. And you learned that when

---

9   Arundhati Roy, "The Pandemic Is a Portal," *Financial Times*, April 3, 2020, https://www.ft.com/content/10d8f5e8-74eb-11ea-95fe-fcd274e920ca

times are tough, you cannot just bear down, work through it the best you can, and return to normal, whatever that was. You learned that you will (and must) have a new normal. You must adapt and change. Or die. You must use the opportunities presented to you as portals to the future state, to the next normal.

Nothing changes until somebody feels something.

—GAPINGVOID

Let me ask you this. How would you answer these questions? Take these questions into your next leadership or stakeholder meeting and have attendees complete this; find it at AnnetteFranz.com. How will your responses vary from theirs?

CHANGE ASSESSMENT	YOUR THOUGHTS
What's dragging your company down?	
What are your company's pain points? What keeps you up at night?	
What hurt the business the most as the pandemic dragged on?	
What was your greatest learning about the business and the need to do things differently?	
What business situation is your portal from current state to future state?	
Given the chance (and you have that chance every day), how would you start over and build your business differently?	

As I begin transformation work with new clients, I like to ask the questions above. I want to understand the catalyst for change. I want to know the pain that is being felt that is driving the desire to change. I want to identify either the desired outcomes or which *un*desirable outcomes are being avoided. And I want to know that the appetite for change is real (i.e., there is pain, and there is a sense of urgency). The answers are usually something along the lines of "We're losing customers" or "Our revenue is down" or "Employee churn is through the roof." I then ask them, "How will you do things differently going forward and keep from returning to business as usual?" Suddenly, change becomes mission critical. But … *nothing changes if nothing changes.*

As I outline their strategies for the change that lies ahead, I repeat this mantra to them: nothing changes if nothing changes. It seems silly to say, but it's necessary. Oddly and unfortunately, it's a rude awakening for some leaders, while it chastises others with an anxiety about change. Leaders expect things to be done differently, but they do nothing to ensure that change really takes place. What's happening there?

WHY NOTHING CHANGES

Well, there are a lot of reasons (excuses) change doesn't happen. **Fear of change** is probably the top—or one of the top—reasons. What kind of fear? Fear of what will happen. You don't know what you don't know, but you won't know until you try. But you can't try because you're afraid to. This is an issue for both leaders and employees. When it comes to changing your culture to be one that is customer-centric, the one thing you need to pose to yourself, the one thing that will calm the fear of change—or drive you mad with "Why haven't we changed?"—is this: imagine the business if there were no customers.

Another reason leaders don't want to initiate change is that **they don't believe in it**. They don't think it will make a difference. And ego often plays a huge role: "We don't need to change. I've set us up for success. We're doing just fine." I've seen this time and time again. Customer experience professionals have to prove the return on investment (ROI) of improving the customer experience, of putting the customers at the heart of the business, when, ultimately, you're in business for and because of customers, so why wouldn't you put them at the center of the business? Why would there be any doubt that being customer-driven and customer-obsessed is great for the business?

Change initiatives also don't get off the ground when leaders feel that change might have **worked for others but won't work for them**. "That's not for us. We're different." While it's true that you can't replicate the culture of Zappos or any other business, you can certainly do the same work they're doing or have done to make their cultures centered on the customer. Your business is different, no doubt. But it's not unique in that it, like others, is based on employees building your products and customers buying those products, products that solve problems for them. As you continue through this book, you'll learn what it is that other companies do—and what you must do.

Oh, and **change is hard** is another excuse that gets bandied about. I think I've already addressed that one earlier in the chapter, but let's just solidify and amplify this point: if you can pivot to survive during a pandemic, you can pivot to survive any time. Changing your culture to be customer-centric is change for good, change for survival. Don't discount it as hard. Embrace it as a must—a must if you want to lead a winning organization.

And finally, **change fatigue** (see the sidebar box, "Change Fatigue Is Real") is a real issue that keeps future change initiatives from getting off the ground. It's an organizational affliction that makes people weary and wary of change. According to Wikipedia:[10] *Organizational*

---

10 "Organizational Change Fatigue," Wikipedia, accessed November 30, 2021, https://en.wikipedia.org/wiki/Organizational_change_fatigue

change fatigue is a general sense of apathy or passive resignation toward organizational changes by individuals or teams. Organizational change efforts are all too often unfocused, uninspired, and unsuccessful. Research shows, 70 percent of transformation efforts fail, often caused by change fatigue. Where does change fatigue come into the picture? Well, with the "been there, done that" experience and attitude, for starters. Especially when change initiatives constantly fail, there's this sense that each initiative is a "flavor of the month" and a waste of time and effort.

> *The more change is pushed on employees, the more they push back, especially when change is random and unclear.*

I'm here to tell you again: you *know* you need to change. And nothing changes if nothing changes. For your business, that change starts with the culture. We know that leaders get what they allow, especially when it comes to culture. That's often how a corporate culture, when not deliberately defined and designed, gets established. In order to deliberately make a change, know that it requires an adjustment of both mindset and behaviors—for leaders first and then for employees.

> *Faced with the choice between changing one's mind and proving that there is no need to do so, almost everyone gets busy on the proof.*

—JOHN KENNETH GALBRAITH,
PROFESSOR OF ECONOMICS, HARVARD UNIVERSITY

FORCE FIELD ANALYSIS

Want to understand what's driving or what's impeding change in your organization? Use Lewin's force field analysis to get a better understanding of those forces for and against change to define how you'll communicate to not only bring along the detractors but also amplify the promoters of the change and to make decisions that will ultimately help to make the change palpable to everyone in the organization.

Here's what the force field analysis looks like.

FORCE FIELD ANALYSIS

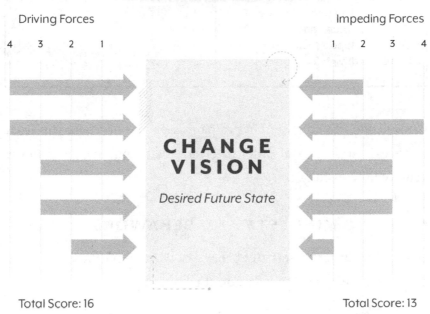

Driving Forces

4 3 2 1

CHANGE VISION

Desired Future State

Impeding Forces

1 2 3 4

Total Score: 16   Total Score: 13

To build it out, start with outlining your change vision or your desired future state. In this case, you're looking to change the culture to one that is customer-centric. Then capture forces that drive and support this change, followed by those things that impede or obstruct the change. Next, score each of those forces on a scale of one to five, where one is weak and five is strong. You can find this assessment at AnnetteFranz.com.

Now it's time to analyze each of the forces based on their scores:

FORCE FIELD ANALYSIS	YOUR THOUGHTS
Which driving forces offset the impeding forces?	
Which impeding forces are detrimental to the desired outcome?	
Which impeding forces require training, communication, technology, support, etc. in order to flip them to driving forces?	

Completing this exercise starts to paint a picture of where you need to focus your efforts in order to ensure that your change vision is achieved successfully.

SHIFTING MINDSETS AND BEHAVIORS

In order to shift mindsets and behaviors, whether it's those of leaders or of employees, you'll need to do the following:

- Make sure that everyone knows the purpose, the vision, the goals, and the desired outcomes—and that they understand the why behind all of it—to create a "greater cause" mentality.
- Be clear on what you are changing to; in other words, what is the current state, and what is the desired future state?
- Know and understand your audience: How do they learn? What motivates them?
- Involve the audience, and make sure they know what it means for them and what's in it for them.
- Frame the proposed shift in a way that they'll understand.
- Create context and tell a story; stories are a Trojan horse for learning.

- Build your business case.
- Start small and show some quick wins to help build momentum, to help get people on board (it won't happen all at once).
- Communicate clearly, openly, candidly, and regularly.
- Regularly reinforce and reaffirm the change.
- And don't forget to communicate what happens if you don't change.

Back in 2015, McKinsey reported[11] that "at companies where senior managers communicate openly and across the organization about the transformation's progress, respondents are 8.0 times as likely to report a successful transformation as those who say this communication doesn't happen. Good communication has an even greater effect at enterprise-wide transformations, where company-wide change efforts are 12.4 times more likely to be successful when senior managers communicate continually."

No one can be forced to change. The secret to change is to involve the people who are affected by the change in the change process. But as a leader, before you involve people, *you* need to believe in it first—and shift your mindset and your behaviors. I can't force you to change your culture as a result of reading this book, but I'm going to make that change compelling, and I'm going to help you understand what it means for the business and why it's important. The rest is up to you.

But in the end, I have no doubt in my mind that culture change is required of many brands today, and those who won't change eventu-

---

11   "How to beat the transformation odds," McKinsey & Company, April 1, 2015, https://www.mckinsey.com/business-functions/organization/our-insights/how-to-beat-the-transformation-odds

ally have to make some adjustments or suffer the consequences. This is what happened to Starbucks.

TO SAVE THE BUSINESS, STARBUCKS
RETURNS TO ITS ROOTS[12]

Howard Schultz, former CEO of Starbucks, has said, "The only thing we have is one another. The only competitive advantage we have is the culture and values of the company. Anyone can open up a coffee store. We have no technology. We have no patent. All we have is the relationship around the values of the company and what we bring to the customer every day. And we all have to own it."

On February 14, 2007, a memo that he had written to his leadership team (he was chairman at the time) was leaked, and the world got a peek into some of the issues Starbucks was facing. The memo starts off with the following:

"Over the past ten years, in order to achieve the growth, development, and scale necessary to go from less than 1,000 stores to 13,000 stores and beyond, we have had to make a series of decisions that, in retrospect, have led to the watering down of the Starbucks experience, and, what some might call the commoditization of our brand."

Ouch.

In an interview years later, he said he wrote the memo because he felt Starbucks was measuring and rewarding the wrong activities and behaviors and was no longer focused on customers or employees. Instead, they were focused on growth, which in some regards was masking what was really happening on the inside. "Growth became

---

12   Mike Hofman, "Memo to Howard Schultz … ," *Inc.*, March 3, 2007, https://www.inc.com/staff-blog/2007/03/07/memo_to_howard_schultz.html

a virus within the company, and in many ways, it began to cover up mistakes."

He went on to say that it wasn't one thing but a series of things that prompted him to write that memo. At that time, the stock price was at an all-time high, but as he notes, a company can't be defined by its stock price but rather by its relationship with its customers, its purpose, its values, and its guiding principles. After the memo, he discovered through a series of results that "the underbelly of the company was not as healthy as it once was." At that point, he knew the only way to set the ship right was to return the company to its core values—and to investing in their people.

He subsequently brought together eleven thousand company leaders and shared that, critical to righting the ship, it was essential to not think of the business in terms of growth and volume and numbers but to shift the mindset to one store, one partner, one extraordinary cup of coffee, and the mission of exceeding the expectations of every customer—with the recognition that they can't exceed the expectations of the customer if they don't exceed the expectations of their employees (partners). He promised to transform the company financially but shared that it would not be a success if the people are left behind. It would have to "be done in a way in which the culture and the values of the company are embraced, preserved, and enhanced."

If you don't like change, you're going to like irrelevance even less.

—GENERAL ERIC SHINSEKI

BACK TO SHIFTING MINDSETS AND BEHAVIORS

I also have no doubt that many company *leaders* need to change. If they don't, they will be pushed out. An organization cannot change without its leaders being on board and in alignment with the change. An organization cannot change if its leaders are the reason it needs to change. You'll learn more about that in chapter 4. But if leaders are not going to get *on* the bus, then they need to get *off* the bus for the sake of the business. I implore you to stay on the bus and build a winning organization that you and others can be proud of.

It was Einstein who said, "We can't solve problems by using the same kind of thinking we used when we created them." This is true. We need to do things differently in order to do things differently. So yes, change is not only necessary but also critical to success; it is also inevitable—with or without your involvement. So make the decision to change. Make it a deliberate change.

DEFINING YOUR CHANGE VISION

Once you've accepted the fact that you need to make a change, in order to start down the change path, you need to bring along the people who will be impacted. The first step is to create and define a vision for this change. A change vision is a statement or image of some desired future state (i.e., what the company will look like after you change), along with details about why this future state is desirable. It will give employees a sense of the magnitude of the change and the overall impact on the organization.

> **We need to do things differently in order to do things differently.**

John Kotter, the master guru of change management, states that a change vision serves three purposes:

1. It simplifies and clarifies the outcome of the change.
2. It motivates people to make the change.
3. It aligns individuals around the goal or outcome, giving them a shared sense of direction.

Communicating your vision is an important piece of change management. If no one knows what it is or why it's taking place, then people start to ignore it; they certainly don't want to be a part of it. Of course, the key is to communicate the right information. Early. And often. Keep communicating.

Employees want to know the following:

- What's changing?
- Why is it changing?
- How long will it take?
- What's the impact on the business?
- What does it mean for me?
- What's my role?
- What's in it for me?
- What happens if I don't get involved?
- What happens if I don't change?
- What happens if we (the company) don't change?

The things you talk about regularly and repeatedly are deemed important by your employees.

Kotter outlines seven key elements to effectively communicate your change vision.[13] They include the following:

1. **Keep it simple:** don't use jargon and language that is confusing to those who need to understand it.

2. **Use metaphors, analogies, and examples:** paint a picture of what the current state is and what the future state will be. Tell stories about where you came from, where you are today, and where you're headed.

3. **Use multiple forums:** there are different channels and methods to communicate the vision, including meetings, town halls, memos, emails, conversations, etc.

4. **Be repetitive:** it will really sink in when employees hear the vision over and over again.

5. **Lead by example:** executives and leaders must be the role models for the change they expect to see; their behaviors cannot be inconsistent with the change vision.

6. **Explain seeming inconsistencies:** if inconsistencies go unaddressed, they will derail the whole effort and kill the credibility of the entire change effort.

7. **Give and take:** use two-way communication; don't just talk, listen. Employees will have questions and feedback. Listen, answer, and address.

I would add that you should message with empathy and caring. Don't dictate. Don't ram it down their throats. Communicate in a way that lets people know not only that it's important but that so are they and their feelings and perspectives about the change.

---

13   "Kotter's Leading Change Step 4 Communicating the Vision," Maciver Project
     Services, accessed November 30, 2021, https://www.maciverprojectservices.co.uk/2010/
     kotters-leading-change-step-4-communicating-the-vision/

Vision without action is a daydream. Action without vision is a nightmare.

Of course, you can have the most amazing change vision in the world, but if you don't actually execute on it, you lose credibility, and you lose a great opportunity to improve the experience for employees and for customers. There's a Japanese proverb that states: "Vision without action is a daydream. Action without vision is a nightmare." You can't really have one without the other. Set your vision. Outline the strategy to achieve it. And go do it.

That's a great segue to the next chapter, in which I begin taking you through the ten foundational principles of a customer-centric culture. These are the various components that are necessary to have in place in order to change your business into a winning organization.

Remember this: change is possible. (Yes, it's hard work.) It's a matter of choice. It's about priorities. It requires understanding and focus. It requires leadership. It's a mindset shift first, then a behavior shift. It means thinking (and then doing) differently. It's short-term pain for long-term gains.

The bottom line: You'll change when you want to. You'll change when you need to. You'll change when the pain is so bad that all you can do is change. You'll change because it's the right thing to do. Or your business will die/fail.

Survival of the fittest. You got this.

DO YOU SEE ...	WHAT TO DO?	OUTCOMES OR BENEFITS
Excuses being made for why the business can't change?	Listen. Understand. Outline and communicate the change vision. Help folks understand outcomes of change versus no change.	Clarity. Understanding. Updated change plan. Alignment.
Change fatigue?	Share quick wins, and celebrate progress and successes. Talk about progress regularly.	Employees keep the faith and don't feel like it's another "flavor of the month" initiative.
A misunderstood change vision?	Simplify the vision. Tell the change story. Break it into the following: What? Why? Outcomes? What if we don't change?	Clarity and alignment.

CHANGE FATIGUE IS REAL

In October 2020, Jessica Knight, vice president at Gartner, noted, "The amount of change[14] that the average employee can absorb without becoming fatigued is half what it was last year. Employees' ability to absorb change has plummeted precisely at the time when more organizations need change to reset."

I recently worked with a client whose employees experienced change fatigue. They couldn't handle any additional ideas or initiatives to change the business because there were so many already underway, yet so few, if any, of these "grand announcements" ever amounted to anything.

Why does change fatigue happen?

- There's a nonstop flow of change initiatives.
- Many of them are flavors of the month or reactionary, with no thought given to long-term strategy and goals.
- Each one requires employees to do more work—work they view as superfluous—on top of their already hectic workloads.
- Many initiatives don't have clear owners, objectives, or outcomes.
- Or the importance, purpose, and outcomes are not clearly communicated to the team or to all employees.
- But the change is all leaders talk about.

---

14   Dave Howard, "Embrace Change? Disruption Fatigue Is Beating Us Down," Medium, February 21, 2021, https://medium.com/dont-make-me-think/embrace-change-disruption-fatigue-is-beating-us-down-89f13f21a961

HOW DO YOU KNOW CHANGE FATIGUE HAS SET IN?

- Employees are skeptical when any new initiative is introduced.
- They no longer volunteer to help, participate, or be part of a change project team.
- They view that as a waste of time.
- Employees watch from the sidelines, snickering that this is just another flavor of the month.
- For those who chose to participate, they lose interest and no longer pay attention or actively engage in their piece of the work.
- They've lost sight of the endgame, the outcomes, and the reason for the change.
- Executives start to shift the budget and resources to other initiatives.
- Employees leave the company; too much change creates burnout, havoc, and uncertainty.

HOW CAN YOU MITIGATE THE FATIGUE?

- Talk about it, just not all the time. Be transparent. Convey important information. And then let the work get done.
- Share quick wins, and celebrate successes along the way so that people know that real change is happening and having a positive impact.
- Revisit objectives and desired outcomes to make sure everything is still on track.

- Remind those involved about the endgame and its benefits.
- Chunk up the change into major milestones. Work toward the milestones, and then celebrate reaching each one.
- Swap out the teams. Bring in new people, if needed.
- Offer incentives for staying with the plan. Nothing perks up a tired team like money or some other incentive. But remember that the incentive must be tied to the right behavior and to the desired outcome. Don't incentivize for the sake of it. Make it meaningful, and make sure it's linked to the change you want to achieve.
- Remind everyone why change is happening and who it impacts. Tell the story.

CHAPTER 3

Principle 1—Culture Is the Foundation

Over time, I have come to view culture as the fundamental defining element of the workplace. If the work is what an organization does, workplace culture is how an organization does it.

—JOHNNY C. TAYLOR JR., PRESIDENT AND CEO OF
THE SOCIETY FOR HUMAN RESOURCE MANAGEMENT

Zappos isn't the poster child for culture—specifically a customer-centric culture—for nothing. As CEO, Tony Hsieh deliberately built the company and designed the culture to be exactly as it is. In his Stanford Graduate School of Business presentation in 2010, he stated[15] that customer service isn't what's most important to Zappos. Instead, "Our number one priority is company culture. Our whole belief is that if you get the culture right, most of the other stuff like delivering great customer service or building a long-term enduring brand will just happen naturally on its own." He also believed that culture and brand are two sides of the same coin, with brand being a lagging indicator of the culture.

---

15   Neil Patel, "Tony Hsieh, Zappos, and the Art of Great Company Culture," neilpatel.com, accessed November 30, 2021, https://neilpatel.com/blog/zappos-art-of-culture/

Culture is so important for Zappos that they both hire and fire based on whether someone is a culture fit. (More on culture fit in chapter 5.) In other words, they don't care if you are the most skilled person to do the job; if you're not a fit for the Zappos culture, you will either not be hired, or if by luck you slip through the cracks, you'll eventually be fired. They even offer $2,000 to employees during their initial weeks of training to quit if they don't feel the culture is for them. This is how they protect their culture. That's how important it is.

If it seems odd that "culture is the foundation" is the first principle or tenet upon which a customer-centric organization is built, it's not. I don't believe everyone views customer-centricity as something that flows through the organization's DNA, as I noted in chapter 1.

Culture is so important for Zappos that they both hire and fire based on whether someone is a culture fit.

To paint a clear picture of culture's impact on the organization and its criticality to building a winning organization, I've put together this diagram on the opposite page to reflect the linkage between culture, the employee experience, and employee outcomes, customer outcomes, and business outcomes. Your culture, what's happening on the inside, certainly impacts what is seen and felt on the outside. Culture and brand (including your employer brand and your ability to attract strong candidates) are linked for sure, or as Tony Hsieh said, they are two sides of the same coin. I'll go into more detail about this graphic in chapter 13 when I cover linking culture to outcomes.

LINKING EMPLOYEE EXPERIENCE TO OUTCOMES

FOUNDATION

Culture = Values + Behaviors
Leadership Behavior and Actions
Soft Stuff
Hard Stuff

EMPLOYEE EXPERIENCE

Purpose	Valued
Alignment	Appreciated
Belonging	Energy & Enthusiasm
Achievement	

EMPLOYEE OUTCOMES

Engagement	Loyalty
Happiness	(Retention & Advocacy)
Productivity	Creativity
Quality	Innovation

CUSTOMER OUTCOMES

Better Experience
Value Received
Happiness
Satisfaction
Loyalty

BUSINESS OUTCOMES

Employer Branding	Revenue
Recruiting Cycles	Profitability
Competitive Advantage	CLV
Growth	

So what is culture?

Culture is the soul of the organization, truly the foundation. Culture is best defined as "core values + behaviors" and is often described as "how we do things around here." Herb Kelleher, cofounder and former CEO of Southwest Airlines, came up with my favorite definition: **culture is what people do when no one is looking**.

Culture is the organization's DNA. And when we build customer-centricity into the culture, it becomes the soul of the organization. It becomes how we do things around here (i.e., we put the customer at the heart of the business, no questions asked).

Core values are really the beliefs of the organization or, more specifically, of the people who comprise the organization. Without them, employees (and leaders) go about their days without a north star or a guiding light to make sure they always know what's right and what's wrong. Core values guide them in terms of how to interact with each other and with customers.

Culture is best defined as "core values + behaviors" and is often described as "how we do things around here."

One of the best pieces of advice that Brian Chesky,[16] cofounder and CEO of Airbnb, got about culture was from Peter Thiel after he invested $150 million in Airbnb in 2012. Peter's words were simple: "Don't fuck up the culture." Employees love to tout how great Airbnb's culture is, and Peter was no exception; the culture is the reason he invested in Airbnb.

Later, in a letter to employees in which he shared Peter's advice, Brian noted, "The culture is what creates the foundation for all future

---

16   Brian Chesky, "Don't Fuck Up the Culture," Medium, April 20, 2014, https://medium.com/@bchesky/dont-fuck-up-the-culture-597cde9ee9d4

innovation. If you break the culture, you break the machine that creates your products."

He went on to say, "Why is culture so important to a business? Here is a simple way to frame it. The stronger the culture, the less corporate process a company needs. When the culture is strong, you can trust everyone to do the right thing."

But what happens when your executives' and your employees' behaviors don't align with your values? What happens when that trust is broken? Bad things. Here are some examples, going back to the financial crisis of 2007–2008.

- Consider **Enron**. Enron's core values were integrity, communication, respect, and excellence. But their leaders destroyed the company and went to jail for fraud.
- I've searched for **MCI WorldCom's** values, but the company is gone, and so are any traces of their core values.
- I couldn't find **Lehman Brothers'** values either, but I found plenty of articles talking about their toxic culture. And I did find an article stating that executives and employees were rewarded for taking risks—at all costs. That led to fudging the books as well. So integrity and ethical behaviors went out the window.
- If you take a look at **Goldman Sachs's** principles and standards, you'll see the first one states that they do everything in the best interest of their customers—and the last one on the page is all about honesty and integrity. And yet they admitted to defrauding investors in 2008.
- **Merrill Lynch's** principles, which were replaced by Bank of America's core values when they acquired Merrill Lynch, were all about teamwork, client focus, integrity, and more. Merrill

Lynch was headed in the same direction as Lehman Brothers because it carried a lot of the same toxic debt/assets.

What's my point?

It's not to belabor the mistakes of those who failed—and failed badly.

The point is this: **values are meaningless unless they inspire and drive the behavior that you expect your employees and executives (they're not exempt!) to display**. In other words, your core values mean nothing if everyone in the company doesn't live them.

It's not hard to make decisions when you know what your values are.

—ROY DISNEY

If you don't know your company's values, if they aren't a driving force behind your culture—or if you don't believe they are the soul of your organization—it's time to dust them off and put them in the spotlight where they belong.

Danny Meyer, CEO of Union Square Hospitality Group,[17] has said, "It's the job of any business owner to be clear about the company's non-negotiable core values. They're the riverbanks that help guide us as we refine and improve on performance and excellence. A lack of riverbanks creates estuaries and cloudy waters that are confusing to navigate. I want a crystal-clear, swiftly-flowing stream."

> **The culture is a mess. Employees are not aligned. The business suffers.**

---

17   "The 5 Habits of Quality-Focused Companies," *Inc.*, accessed November 30, 2021, https://www.inc.com/guides/201101/five-habits-of-quality-focused-companies.html

Don't have any core values? Get the important task of developing them on the docket right away. And by the way, that explains a lot: it's why your workplace feels so disjointed. I've seen it happen both at companies for which I've worked and with client organizations. The culture is a mess. Employees are not aligned. The business suffers.

Let me ask you some questions about your company's core values. Share this assessment with the entire leadership team; you can find it at AnnetteFranz.com. If you don't know the answers, please reach out to your human resources (HR) department to get them. If they don't know the answers, you might be in trouble.

CORE VALUES ASSESSMENT	YOUR RESPONSES
Do your core values support the type of culture you want in your organization (e.g., customer-centric, collaborative, innovative, inclusive, etc.)?	
Who created the core values in your business?	
What was the process to identify and to finalize them?	
Have acceptable and unacceptable behaviors for each value been outlined?	
Have they ever changed?	
If so, why?	
How are they socialized?	
Are they simply posters on a wall?	
Are they taught in orientation?	
Do leaders in the organization model the values?	
Is there ongoing core values training?	
Are core values talked about in meetings?	
How are they operationalized?	
Are they used during the interview process?	

Are they used for hiring and firing decisions?	
Are they a factor in promotion decisions?	
Are they taken into account when you develop policies or processes or make decisions?	
How are the values reinforced?	
Are employees recognized for living the values, either by their managers or their peers?	
Are they part of performance reviews?	
How do the values support customer-centricity, collaboration, and diversity and inclusion?	

DESIGNING THE DESIRED CULTURE

This book is about building a winning organization through a customer-centric culture. So keep this in mind: you've got to have the core values in place to support a customer-centric culture. You must deliberately design a culture of customer-centricity. And that only happens when there's a commitment from the top to put the customer and the customer experience front and center.

Culture is like the wind. It is invisible; yet its effect can be seen and felt.

—BRYAN WALKER, PARTNER AND

MANAGING DIRECTOR, IDEO

The graphic on the next page is an easy way to illustrate what it takes to design your desired culture. Start by defining the culture you want, then identify core values that align with that culture, outline the respective behaviors, align the values to the desired outcomes, and finally, socialize and operationalize the values.

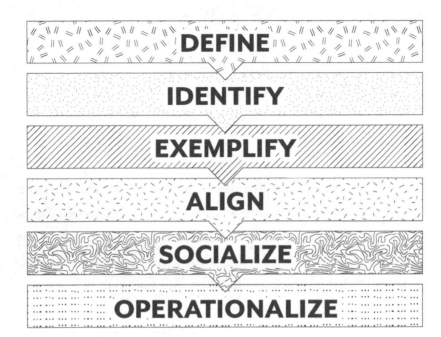

DEFINE

IDENTIFY

EXEMPLIFY

ALIGN

SOCIALIZE

OPERATIONALIZE

DEFINE
Define the culture you desire for your organization

IDENTIFY
Identify your core values and the values that align with your
culture definition; evaluate mission, vision & purpose to ensure alignment

EXEMPLIFY
For each core value, outline the behaviors that exemplify the value

ALIGN
Align each value with an outcome if it is intended to
deliver for the organization

SOCIALIZE
Prepare a plan for how you'll communicate values through the organization

OPERATIONALIZE
Design the culture. Coach and train on how to put each value into action
to achieve your desired outcomes

VALUES SHIFT THE CULTURE

In chapter 1, I offered some examples of customer-centric values (e.g., we listen, deliver *wow* through service, customer obsession, focus on the customer and all else will follow, strong relationships create guests for life, customer trust, and more). I want to share a story with you about the last one, customer trust, in order to illustrate the importance and the impact of these core values.

I had been working with a client when it surfaced that customer trust was a major issue they were facing day in and day out. We did a lot of work around what that meant for both the business and the customer and did a root cause analysis to get to the heart of the matter. Whenever customers called with issues, there seemed to be this butting of heads between agents and customers. Employees pushed back on customers because they didn't believe them; they felt customers were always calling to just get something for nothing.

We took a step back and looked at their core values. They didn't have one that was clearly tied to the customer experience. In the end, we decided to add a new core value: customer trust. We defined what it meant and what behaviors were aligned and not aligned with it. We helped employees understand what it meant and how to operationalize it.

What happened next was amazing. The client said in her own words: "Everything just became easier. It was just there. It had never been there before." In other words, it's how they do business now. Everyone knows what's right and wrong. And it's all just easier. No questions asked. Customers were no longer questioned or interrogated. They were simply trusted. What a shift in experience for both employees and customers.

This is why I say that culture is the foundation. A great culture leads to great outcomes.

Don't believe it?

LSA Global conducted organizational alignment research[18] and found that culture accounts for 40 percent of the difference between high- and low-performing organizations when it comes to revenue growth, profitability, customer loyalty, leadership effectiveness, and employee engagement.

Watson Wyatt found[19] that culturally aligned organizations return 286 percent more value to stakeholders, while *Harvard Business Review* reported that as much as 50 percent of the competitive difference between companies in the same industry can be attributed to culture.

Culture is the optimal performance driver. It is an unsigned contract between an organization and its employees that gives individuals license to accomplish goals and get things done without the burden of worry or uncertainty about negative repercussions. And every employee in an organization has the power to amplify or detract from its culture.

—GALLUP

Amen to that! What a powerful statement!

---

18   "Why It is Important to Have a Clear Company Culture," LSA Global, accessed November 30, 2021, https://lsaglobal.com/blog/why-it-is-important-to-have-a-clear-company-culture/

19   "A Misaligned Workplace Culture Creates Problems," LSA Global, accessed November 30, 2021, https://lsaglobal.com/blog/a-misaligned-workplace-culture-creates-problems/

WD-40 LIVES, BREATHES, AND PLAYS BY THEIR VALUES[20]

Garry Ridge, CEO of WD-40, is a huge proponent of building a strong culture for business success, so much so that on the WD-40 website, with each job posting, there's a statement that reads: "Please, only consider employment with WD-40 Company if you feel as strongly about our values as we do: We live, breathe, and play by our values every day."

Those values are listed hierarchically:

1. We value doing the right thing.
2. We value creating positive, lasting memories in all our relationships.
3. We value making it better than it is today.
4. We value succeeding as a tribe while excelling as individuals.
5. We value owning it and passionately acting on it.
6. We value sustaining the WD-40 Company economy.

Garry knows that defining and living the values is at the heart of a winning business. He also knows that customers, not shareholders, are the top priority. He spoke in an interview in January 2021 about how expectations for a publicly traded company are to make money. But the number one and two core values for WD-40 are, as listed above, "we value doing the right thing" and "we value creating positive, lasting memories in all our relationships."

---

20   Ayse Birsel, "WD-40 Does $380 Million in Sales a Year. Its Secret Sauce is Surprisingly Simple," *Inc.*, accessed November 30, 2021, https://www.inc.com/ayse-birsel/how-wd-40-does-380-million-in-sales-a-year-by-living-these-3-key-values.html

Values in an organization are there to set us free, not to in any way restrict us from what we do.

—GARRY RIDGE

The following is an example he shared about how WD-40 lives its values. They have a rule in the company that no Prop. 65 cancer-causing chemicals can be used in anything they make. While they know they could be more profitable if they used some of these chemicals, like their competitors do, they choose not to because of these two values, leaving money on the table as a result because they live their values.

To win in the marketplace, you must first win in the workplace.

—DOUG CONANT

CULTURE: THE GLUE OR THE UNGLUE

When I first start working with a new client, I like to interview executives and a sampling of both employees and customers. I ask executives and employees alike the following three questions about culture.

1. In a few keywords, how would you describe your culture?
2. What is the glue that holds the company together? (This one always gets a "That's a good question" response.)
3. What is the unglue? What breaks the company apart?

The responses are always interesting. And rarely are the answers that employees offer up all that different from what executives say. There's definitely overlap. And that begs the question, If you all know what the problems are, why aren't you fixing them? Reread chapter 2 to put the fear of change behind you! Or carry on to chapter 4 to learn more about your role as a leader in creating a customer-centric organization.

DO YOU SEE ...	WHAT TO DO?	OUTCOMES OR BENEFITS
No customer-driven core values?	Add a core value that embodies the customer-driven behaviors you'd like to see.	It's not hard to make decisions when you know your values. Customer-centric culture. Better customer experience.
Behaviors haven't been outlined for core values?	Engage your culture committee (see chapter 10) to take on this task as outlined in chapter 1.	Employees know right from wrong. You can rest assured that they will know what to do when no one is looking.
Values haven't been socialized and/or operationalized?	Develop a plan to communicate and activate your values. And execute.	The culture you desire.

CHAPTER 4

Principle 2—Leadership Commitment and Alignment Are Critical to Success

The culture of any organization is shaped by the worst behavior the leader is willing to tolerate.

—STEVE GRUENERT AND TODD WHITAKER,
SCHOOL CULTURE REWIRED

Chick-fil-A is a successful brand and a customer-centric organization that lives its core values. Of particular importance to Chick-fil-A is collaboration and customer orientation, both of which are at the heart of customer-centricity. Their core values (from their website) are as follows:

- **We're here to serve.** We keep the needs of Operators, their Team Members and customers at the heart of our work, doing what is best for the business and best for them.
- **We're better together.** It's through teamwork and collaboration that we do our best work. We're an inclusive culture that leverages the strengths of our diverse talent to innovate and maximize our care for Operators, their Team Members and customers.

- **We are purpose-driven.** We model our Purpose every day, connecting our work and daily activities to our business strategy, supporting each other's efforts to be good stewards who create positive impact on all who come in contact with Chick-fil-A.
- **We pursue what's next.** We find energy in adapting and reinventing how we do things, from the way we work to how we care for others.

For CEO Dan Cathy, it wasn't enough to tell employees that they must put their families first when they make decisions about their work-life balance; instead, he realized that if he wanted to make a real impact, if he wanted them to believe what he was preaching, he would have to be the example. Whenever his kids had sporting events, he made it a point to leave the office midday to attend the games. But he didn't just leave the office out the back door; he did so in a very public way, down the building's central staircase—just to make the point. He modeled the behavior he wanted to see from his staff and from the rest of the employees.

Another CEO who gets this concept is Troy Aikman. I'm sure when you hear that name, the first thing you think of is football, but Troy is also a businessman—and not just any businessman but a sharp-dressed one. When it came to work/business, he was (and is) always well groomed and wearing a suit.

A couple of years back, I was attending a client's annual customer event, and they hosted Troy Aikman as a keynote fireside chat. During that chat, he shared the story of when he bought his first car dealership. Shortly after the purchase, he walked into the building and noticed that all of the sales guys (yes, all men) were dressed in business casual (i.e., polo shirts and slacks). He wanted them to dress nicer, but he didn't want to come into his new business and be a hardnose right away, so he didn't say anything. Instead, he just showed up at the dealership every day wearing a suit. By the end of the first week, a couple of the guys had clued in and upgraded their attire, and by the end of the second week, all of them were dressed in suits. And he never said a word!

It's a great reminder that you can drive change—lasting change—when you do a few simple, yet often forgotten, things. Troy didn't talk about any conversations he had with the staff after the two weeks, but I can only imagine he applauded their actions.

To deliberately design the culture that you want and to drive lasting change, do the following:

- **Communicate** the change using a variety of channels and media. Share the change vision. Tell the change story. Let employees know what is changing, why it's changing, how it will impact them and what they do (differently) on a daily basis, and how they will be involved. While Troy chose not to do this, it's so important; you're not a celebrity, so do the work! If no one knows what the change is or why it's taking place, then they'll ignore it; they certainly don't want to be a part of it. *Plus, the things you talk about regularly are deemed important by your employees.*

- **Involve employees** in the change process rather than forcing change on them. If they're involved, the solutions may be richer because they have other perspectives and experiences that the decision-making leader may not have. Better yet, present them (spoken or unspoken, as was the case with Troy) with a problem or a situation, and let them come to the conclusion themselves. If they believe it was their own idea, it'll stick; they'll own it.

- It's important that executives **lead by example and model the change** that they wish to see from their employees; if they don't live the change, why should employees?! If your CEO doesn't demonstrate commitment to the transformation by being the role model for how to deliver a great experience, it won't happen. If she doesn't live the core values, why should you? Actions always speak louder than words.

- **Recognize the right behaviors and reinforce** with incentives, promotions, metrics, and more. Reinforcing the behaviors, actions, and changes that you want to see is more powerful than talking about them, especially when combined with modeling them.

Leaders play a huge role in organizational change, in living the values and designing the culture they desire, in building a customer-centric organization. Back in chapter 1, I mentioned that a customer-centric culture is deliberately designed to be that way. It doesn't occur by accident. This design comes from the top, from the CEO. The CEO (and the entire executive/leadership team) must be committed to—and aligned on—bringing the customer voice into all they do. The leadership team must communicate to employees what it means to be customer-centric and how it impacts the work they do. That also means that they must lead by example and model customer-centric behaviors.

The culture of the company is the behavior of its leaders. Leaders get the behavior they exhibit and tolerate. You change the culture of a company by changing the behavior of its leaders.

—LARRY BOSSIDY, FORMER CEO OF HONEYWELL

COMMITMENT AND ALIGNMENT

Before I continue, let me take you through a couple of terms I just mentioned that are at the core of this chapter: commitment and alignment.

Let's start with **commitment**, which is not the same as buy-in. Buy-in is weak. It says, "Yeah, I'm interested. Sounds good. I'll support it. I'll be part of it." It sounds as weak as it is, and there's no skin in the game.

> "I'm committed to this. I will do this. I'm in. I'll make it happen."

Commitment, on the other hand, is a promise; you're dedicated, and you have an obligation to carry through. "I'm committed to this. I will do this. I'm in. I'll make it happen." It's strong, and it's what leaders need to do and be. Make a decision. Take a stance. Make it happen.

I like the "6 Key Components of Commitment" as outlined by Janssen Sports Leadership Center:[21] solemn promise, full investment, willingness to sacrifice, long-term obligation, pact to persevere, and agreement to act. Those say it all and clearly define what commitment means.

The story of "The Chicken and the Pig" illustrates the difference. While it compares involvement and commitment, I feel like buy-in is at the involvement level. The story goes like this:

---

21   "The Six Key Components of Commitment," powerbasketball, accessed November 30, 2021, http://www.powerbasketball.com/131001.html#

A chicken and a pig are walking down the road.

The chicken says: "Hey Pig. I was thinking we should open a restaurant."

Pig replies: "Hmm, maybe. What would we call it?"

The Chicken offers: "How about Ham and Eggs?"

The Pig thinks about it for a second and then says: "No, thanks. I'd be committed, but you'd only be involved."

Keep in mind that there's no wishy-washiness in winning organizations. Leaders must *commit* to putting the customer at the heart of the business. That commitment comes not only in a verbal form but also in the form of resources—human, time, capital, etc.—to show employees that "we mean business." Commitment is real; it's tangible.

Let's shift gears to **alignment**. There are a lot of factors that contribute to a leadership team's success, but none are as important as team alignment. This is an important concept to cover because it makes the difference between an enterprise-wide effort and, well, not. I like the *Merriam-Webster* definition of alignment: "the state of being joined with others in supporting or opposing something."

A few years back, I came across a book by Miles Kierson, *The Transformational Power of Executive Team Alignment*. (Please read it. It's so worth the two-hour read that it is!) One of my favorite quotes from the book is "Calling most executive groups teams would be a stretch of imagination since by definition a team is a group of people who are working on some common end together." Ouch. Miles defines alignment as "a relationship to decisions whereby you own them completely. It is also a commitment to have a decision work." And it's a choice. Each individual on the executive team must choose to be aligned.

How do they choose to be (or become) aligned? They talk it out. They discuss the pros and cons. They share their opinions, likes, dislikes, challenges, opportunities, etc. Everyone has a chance to weigh in. But here's what happens in the end, once it's all out on the table: they choose to align. Not everyone may agree; there will still be differences. But they ultimately fall in line with the decision. They've been heard, and they support the final decision. There's no meeting after the meeting. There's no bad-mouthing the decision. The decision made in the room is the decision that gets supported and carried out going forward. That's the power of alignment.

Unfortunately, most executive teams are not in alignment. They don't work as a "team"; they function more as a "working group" or as a "committee." Simon Sinek says that a team is not a group of people who work together but a group of people who trust each other. Trust is key among your executive team, as is psychological safety, or the ability to speak freely without recourse from the person in charge. If your leaders don't feel like they can share an opinion with the CEO without recourse, then there's definitely an issue. And that ends up trickling down to their interactions with their employees. It certainly limits their ability to create an environment that feels safe for employees.

Individual commitment to a group effort—that is what makes a team work, a company work, a society work, a civilization work.

—VINCE LOMBARDI

In business and especially in our customer experience work, we seek alignment—from both executives and employees. Executives must all be on the same page; there must be a unified approach and commitment to the work that lies ahead. At the same time, we've got to bring employees along as well and ensure that everyone is on board to do the work. For employees, this happens most often when they are involved in decisions rather than having the outcomes of the decisions forced on them.

Here's another way to think about alignment. Are you a leader in a multinational organization or an organization with multiple business units? Do you find yourself striving for the "One [insert brand] Way" across the organization? What you're looking for is alignment. You're striving for everyone to be on the same page, executing in the same manner, working toward the same vision and goals—across the board. The only way to do that is to be in alignment—every leader, every department, every business unit.

CEO PERSPECTIVES ON ALIGNMENT

Jeff Bezos thinks about alignment as *disagree and commit*.[22] For him, the outcome looks like "You know what? I really disagree with this, but you have more ground truth than I do. We're going to do it your way. And I promise I will never tell you I told you so."

Steve Jobs viewed it this way.[23] When asked how he resolves conflict among his management team, he replied: "I've never believed in the theory that … 'Come on, buy into the decision. We're all on the same team. You don't agree, but buy into it. Let's go make it happen.' Because what happens is, sooner or later, you're paying somebody to do what they think is right, but then you're trying to get them to do what they think isn't right … I've always felt that the best way is to get everybody in a room and talk it through until you agree." He basically believed

---

22   Jeff Haden, "Jeff Bezos Uses the 'Disagree and Commit' Rule to Overcome an Uncomfortable Truth about Teamwork," *Inc.*, accessed November 30, 2021, https://www.inc.com/jeff-haden/jeff-bezos-uses-disagree-commit-rule-to-overcome-an-uncomfortable-truth-about-teamwork.html

23   "Steve Jobs Very Rare MIT Speech: Explaining His Management Style at Apple and NeXT," Marketing Strategy, uploaded May 27, 2020, https://www.marketingstrategy.com/videos/steve-jobs-very-rare-mit-speech-explaining-his-management-style-at-apple-next/

that he was paying people to not simply do things but to tell him what to do or what should be done. And at any one time, there aren't that many decisions to be made, so get the people together that are critical to the decision, talk it through, put it all out on the table, and align.

Airbnb cofounder Joe Gebbia[24] takes a different approach to having open dialogue and, ultimately, getting alignment. He created a nomenclature (elephants, dead fish, and vomit) for different types of difficult conversations that may turn some off but paints the picture and very clearly defines and delineates what needs to be discussed and why. What type of meeting do we need to have today? Is it a session about:

- **elephants**? The big things everyone knows or worries about, but nobody wants to talk about.
- **dead fish**? The things that happened a while ago that people still aren't over, but they need to get out, and people need to get over them.
- **vomit**? The things people need to say and have someone just sit there and listen without judgment.

Get it out on the table. Be open. Discuss. Disagree. Agree. Commit to the outcome. Move on.

I was recently watching a series on Netflix, *Car Masters: Rust to Riches*, a show about how Gotham Garage in Temecula, California, restores and flips cars. The business model of the shop is based loosely on the concept of "One Red Paperclip" by Kyle MacDonald, who traded up from one red paper clip to a house after fourteen trades over the course of a year. Gotham Garage trades up on cars (usually three) until they find one that will bring them a six-figure payday. In one particular episode, the car they were about to flip could've brought them $200,000 or more,

---

24   "How Airbnb Is Building Its Culture through Belonging," Culture Amp, accessed November 30, 2021, https://www.cultureamp.com/blog/airbnb-building-culture-through-belonging

but they were offered the opportunity to donate it to the Petersen Automotive Museum in Los Angeles. Mark, the owner, knew the value to the business of getting the car into the museum, but he needed his team to be OK with the decision first. As you can imagine, they weren't: a donation to the museum meant no payday for them. Mark started the alignment exercise. He asked them to throw their thoughts out so everyone could hear and discuss them. They talked about pros and cons. And in the end, everyone got on board with the final decision: donate to the museum.

> **Alignment means everyone has weighed in, has been heard, and has chosen to be in it together.**

Why is this important? It's a lot easier to get things done when everyone has had a chance to weigh in and, ultimately, chooses to align. Alignment means everyone has weighed in, has been heard, and has chosen to be in it together. They are all invested in the final decision. That removes any uncertainties about how the outcome will be achieved.

Building a visionary company requires 1 percent vision and 99 percent alignment.

—JIM COLLINS AND JERRY PORRAS

CULTURE ROTS FROM THE HEAD DOWN

Have you heard the saying "A fish rots from the head down?" It means that the problem starts at the top. Your culture rots from the head down too. It means that the problems, failures, issues, toxicity, etc. in your organization—or any organization—start with the leadership team.

Senior leaders and executives: take a good, hard look at how you and your colleagues act, behave, make decisions, walk the walk/talk the talk, live the values, etc. How would you feel if your employees did what you just did? If you say, "I'd feel great!" then kudos to you. But if you scratch your head and think that what you do is fine because you lead a team or lead the company—but you wouldn't want your employees to act the same way—you are wrong. Everyone in your company must live by the same standards, by the same values.

Good or bad, that's how cultures are purposely created. That's how cultures are sustained. That's how cultures are transformed. That's what they mean when they say that you get the culture you create or allow.

Not sure about the negative impact leaders have on the organization? Need some examples of the bad?

- **Uber.** Travis Kalanick's leadership came into question quite often after videos of him arguing with a driver were released. Other examples: he said Uber wasn't responsible if drivers attacked passengers, and he degraded women. His words and his actions drove the Uber "bro culture."
- **WeWork.** A sexual harassment lawsuit from a former employee describes WeWork as having an "entitled, frat-boy culture that permeates from the top down."
- **Wells Fargo.** As CEO John Stumpf testified before the US Senate Committee, he tried to escape blame for the unethical behavior of his employees. Even though he fired more than five thousand of them for creating unauthorized and bogus accounts, it was really the culture that he created that failed. He blamed his employees.
- **Activision Blizzard.** Sexual harassment lawsuits and discrimination claims by employees and by the State of California are all over the news as I write this book. The company's president

was well aware of the situation, as were other executives, and even enabled the behavior that included "cube crawls," groping female employees, and more.

Leaders must model the behavior they want to see—this is where the real culture transformation begins. And if they see behaviors unbecoming of the culture they desire, they must stop them—not enable them. Because, metaphorically speaking, "What's good for the goose (leader) is good for the gander (employee)." In other words, if you as a leader want employees to act a certain way, then you must live the values and lead, model, and show them what the right or acceptable behavior is. And only then does culture become "how employees act when the CEO (or anyone else) isn't looking." Because let's face it: most of the time, the CEO is not there, looking over an employee's shoulders. But if employees see that executives put themselves "above the law," forget it; that's a major culture fail.

The bottleneck is always at the top of the bottle.

—PETER DRUCKER

One last point here. Remember that you also get what you reward. If you reward sales and growth but talk about being customer-obsessed, the behavior you see will still only be sales driven, not customer-driven.

I've been working with a client who exemplifies this. Even after we developed customer personas to begin *customer experience design* work, all they could talk about was how these were personas that they would need to pursue to *build share of wallet*, to drive awareness for, to build out marketing materials for acquisition purposes, etc. But that was only part of it. The other parts that told me that they are sales driven were the commission structure and the fact that one division won't "share" customers with other divisions because it's "my customer," which means it's also "my commission." It's painful to have conversations with these folks, but there are a few executives in the company, after many conversations, who have seen the light and are starting to turn the ship around. It will take time—after all, they've "always been doing things this way."

NETFLIX LIVES ITS VALUES

Patty McCord was chief talent officer at Netflix for fourteen years. She was influential in developing the Netflix culture and helped to create Netflix's popular Culture Deck. In her TED Talk titled "8 Lessons on Building a Company People Enjoy Working For,"[25] she shares the following as lesson six.

"Your company needs to live out its values. I was talking to a company not long ago, to the CEO. He was having trouble because the company was rocky and things weren't getting done on time, and he felt like things were sloppy. This also was a man who, I observed, never showed up to any meeting on time. Ever. If you're part of a leadership team, the most important thing that you can do to 'uphold your values' is to live them. People can't be what they can't see."

CAMPBELL'S SOUP LEADERSHIP REFRESH[26]

In 2001, Doug Conant inherited an iconic brand, Campbell Soup Company. Well, inherited is a bit strong, but he took over as CEO

---

25   Patty McCord, "8 Lessons on Building a Company People Enjoy Working For,"
      TED The Way We Work, accessed November 30, 2021, https://www.ted.com/talks/
      patty_mccord_8_lessons_on_building_a_company_people_enjoy_working_for/transcript

26   Abram Brown, "How Campbell's Soup Went from Stale to Innovative," *Inc.*, accessed November 30, 2021,
      https://www.inc.com/articles/201109/former-campbells-soup-company-ceo-doug-conant.html

of the 132-year-old company. And the company he "inherited" was in shambles. Market value had dropped by half in the year or two leading up to him stepping into this role because of many factors, not the least of which was changing consumer needs and expectations, none of which Campbell's had been staying on top of or investing in.

When asked during an interview by *Inc.* magazine about the first thing that he did when he became CEO, Doug replied, "I had to get the culture back on track, because my observation has been, is, and always will be, that you can't have an organization that consistently delivers innovation unless you have a high level of engagement and a high level of trust. People just won't take risks. And we had an incredibly low-trust culture based on what had happened. To get there, we recognized that we had to change the leadership profile of the company, and we turned over, in the first three years, 300 of the top 350 leaders of the organization—which is to my knowledge unprecedented in the consumer products industry. Of the 300 people we turned over, 150 people were promoted from within, and 150 were hired from outside: people who were high character, high quality."

His actions highlight three important points:

1. If you're not the right leader for where the company needs to go, you have to go.
2. Leaders are not exempt from living the culture; as a matter of fact, they lead it, they model it, and if it's not the culture you need or desire, the business will go awry.
3. Culture is critical, especially an innovative culture.

Guess what? A customer-centric culture is an innovative culture. It has to be. Innovation is an outcome and a benefit of being customer-centric; if you are putting the customer at the heart of your business, you will be, by definition, innovative. Truly innovative because you've got your finger on the pulse of your customer and her needs and expectations—you will listen to and cocreate with her, ensuring that you're finding products to solve problems for customers, not just finding customers for your products.

The impact and the importance of leadership commitment and alignment with regard to establishing a customer-centric organization is unquestionable. Leaders lead. Leaders show the way. They must show the way together, in a united and unified front.

Leadership commitment and alignment is critical to success, but it's just one of the ten principles that must be followed when building a winning organization. Let's move from leaders to their employees—and talk about how critical strong leadership is to the employee experience and how important the employee experience is to the customer experience and beyond.

DO YOU SEE ...	WHAT TO DO?	OUTCOMES OR BENEFITS
Your leadership team not able to drive change?	Help everyone understand. Communicate. Involve. Model. Recognize and reinforce.	Change that's activated and owned.
Can't seem to align on what you're trying to do?	Talk about what it means to disagree and commit. Discuss the issue/idea. Let everyone have a say. Hear the pros and cons.	Feeling heard. Alignment.
Leaders who don't speak up regarding toxic behavior?	Time to have a conversation. Who's modeling this behavior? Is there a "good for thee, not for me" unspoken rule? Eliminate the source.	Get the culture you desire, not the one you allow.

CHAPTER 5

Principle 3—Employees More First

*You don't build a business—you build people—
and then people build your business.*

—ZIG ZIGLAR

Employee experience. It's finally getting the airtime it deserves. Yes, some of that airtime is coming in the form of more consultants talking and writing about it, but the more they do that, the better we're able to spread the word about the importance of employee experience and point companies in the right direction.

I've been talking about employee experience for what seems like forever. For thirty years, I've been telling clients they need to listen to employees, understand the experience, and do something about it. In the early years, they'd say, "We'll focus on employees later." But in the last year or three, it feels like there's a greater understanding of the implications of waiting until later. (It's not perfect, though. I still hear clients say, "Oh, I never thought about that. You're right. It makes sense that the employee experience drives the customer experience.")

It's not just about the impact on the customer experience—it's also and especially about the impact on employees. It's about treating them like humans, not like cogs in the wheels of corporate success, as

Bob Chapman,[27] CEO of Barry-Wehmiller, says. It's ultimately about caring about people like people, taking care of the people who take care of you (the business).

In Jeffrey Pfeffer's book *Dying for a Paycheck*, he cites the following:

"In one survey, 61 percent of employees said that workplace stress had made them sick and 7 percent said they had actually been hospitalized. Job stress costs US employers more than $300 billion annually and may cause 120,000 excess deaths each year. In China, 1 million people a year may be dying from overwork. People are literally dying for a paycheck. And it needs to stop."

Yup, employee experience needs to be put at the top of the priority list. Immediately.

It's summer of 2021 as I write this book, and one of the hot topics coming out of the pandemic is the employee experience. I'll define that clearly in just a minute, but let's start with an interesting story that seems to summarize employee sentiment and concerns in one fell swoop.

"We all quit. Sorry for the inconvenience."[28] That's what the big pylon sign in front of a Burger King in Lincoln, Nebraska, read. The message was intended as an apology to customers, but the store's managers didn't find it so funny.

The pandemic was an eye-opener for both employees and leadership. Leadership suddenly realized they needed to focus on their employees—many of them having been deemed essential during that time—and employees realized that there were other options, options

---

27 Bob Chapman and Raj Sisodia, *Everybody Matters: The Extraordinary Power of Caring for Your People Like Family* (New York: Portfolio Penguin, 2015).

28 Hayley Vaughn and Rima Abdelkader, "We all quit: Burger King staff leaves note to management on store sign," nbcnews.com, July 13, 2021, https://www.nbcnews.com/news/us-news/we-all-quit-burger-king-staff-leaves-note-management-store-n1273869

that meant either better treatment from the existing employer or moving on to bigger and better opportunities elsewhere.

The Burger King employees chose the latter because of their current working conditions. Despite being essential workers, they were treated as far less than that. They were treated poorly by management, were underappreciated, and were constantly understaffed, and they worked in a kitchen so hot that a couple of employees were hospitalized due to dehydration.

Let me just say this, lest there be any doubt in your mind: that is *not* a good employee experience!

Sadly, this same scenario (or similar ones) happens every single day in every single country around the globe. I once worked for a company that had a mass exodus, including me. Guess what? They just hired people to replace us rather than fix the problems. *That* is the disgraceful part. Rather than fixing the root cause, they simply hired unknowing replacements, who left once they, too, discovered the workplace situation was less than ideal.

WHAT IS EMPLOYEE EXPERIENCE?

So let me step back for a moment and define employee experience. **Employee experience** is the sum of all the **interactions** that an employee has with her employer during the duration of the employment relationship. It includes any way the employee "touches" or interacts with the company and vice versa in the course of doing her job. It also includes the **actions and capabilities** that enable her to do her job. And importantly, it includes her **feelings, emotions, and perceptions** of those interactions and capabilities.

Is it benefits and perks? No. Absolutely not. A lot of executives mistakenly think that because they offer free massages and beer on Fridays that they've checked the employee experience box. They have not.

Is it culture? No. Employee experience and culture are two different things, although culture certainly plays into or affects the employee experience, as you saw in the first graphic in chapter 3. Culture is values plus behavior. It's what employees do when no one is looking. It's like the energy or the vibe of the place. Great cultures make for a great experience, no doubt; toxic cultures drain and demoralize and make for a painful employee experience.

Is it employee engagement? No. Employee engagement is an outcome. Engagement comes from within the employee, and yet the company has a role in it as well. When there's some confluence of (1) emotions, commitment, passion, sense of ownership, etc. on the part of the employee about the brand and (2) what the organization does (its mission, purpose, brand promise, employee experience, etc.) to facilitate and enhance those emotions or that commitment, then we have employee engagement.

WHAT COMPRISES EMPLOYEE EXPERIENCE?

Interactions that occur during:	ENABLERS AND/OR BLOCKERS	
	The "Soft Stuff"	The "Hard Stuff"
Interview	Growth & Development	Tools
Job Offer	Feedback & Coaching	Resources
Orientation	Recognition & Appreciation	Policies
Onboarding	Leadership & Care	Processes
Training	Communication	Environmental i.e., workplace / workspace
Doing the Job	Camaraderie & Collaboration	
Performance Feedback	Contributions / Impact / Meaningful Work / Valued	
Life Events	Trust & Respect	
Career Management	Psychological Safety	
Offboarding / Exit	Empowerment	
	Wellness / Wellbeing	
	Purpose / Achievement / Success	

EMPLOYEE INTERACTIONS

The definition of employee experience states that *it's the sum of all the interactions an employee has.* When do these interactions occur? They can occur during any of the following (and more) along the employee/employment life cycle.

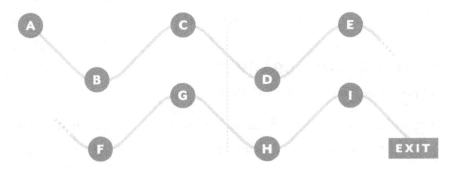

PROCESS

A. Candidate Experience
Application, interview, and job offer — all about first impressions.

B. Orientation
Don't make it all about the company. Include details about the employee, their success, culture, and more.

C. Onboarding
Understanding the role, meeting colleagues, connecting the role to outcomes. Not just hours — spend a week.

D. Training
Ongoing during employment. Invest in employees and help them grow.

E. Doing the Job
Interactions with manager, colleagues, subordinates, executives, customers, vendors, etc.

F. Performance Feedback
Give ongoing feedback, not just during annual performance reviews. Do stay interviews.

G. Life Events
How you treat employees during critical life events (wedding, funerals, birth) shows how much you care.

H. Career Management
Set employee on path to success. Career pathing begins during onboarding.

I. Offboarding & Exit
Make it graceful, easy, and painless — all about last / lasting impressions.

CFO: What happens if we train them and they leave?
CEO: What happens if we don't and they stay?

Be sure to talk to employees about their experience throughout the duration of their employment. Conduct stay interviews rather than exit interviews. Take the time to understand what keeps employees at your company; don't find out when it's too late.

ACTIONS AND CAPABILITIES
THAT ENABLE EMPLOYEES

The definition also talks about actions and capabilities. The actions and capabilities that enable employees to do their jobs can be broken out into the "soft stuff" and the "hard stuff." These not only fill in the cracks of what was just mentioned with regard to employee interactions along the employment life cycle but also address overarching actions and capabilities that must support the employee throughout the duration of employment.

THE SOFT STUFF

The items in the table on the next page are considered the soft stuff, the part of the experience that isn't always tangible, though much of it should be.

Growth and development: Employees and managers must work together on setting career goals, developing a career plan, and working toward it.	**Feedback and coaching:** Managers provide continuous constructive feedback about employee performance, coach them, and help them maintain or improve performance.	**Recognition and appreciation:** Leaders must take the time to recognize employees for living the core values and for the work they do and say "thank you" or show gratitude on a regular basis.
Leadership and care: When leaders embrace servant leadership and/or truly human leadership day in and day out, employees win.	**Communication:** Leaders must be open, honest, candid, and transparent with their communications, whether it's sharing information about the company or about the individual and her performance.	**Camaraderie and collaboration:** Employees should be encouraged to "work together, play together." Leaders must take a real and sincere interest in their staff, getting to know them on a more personal level.
Contributions: Leaders must convey to employees the impact of their work, that they are doing meaningful work, and that their contributions are valued. Ensure they understand the company's "why" and how they contribute.	**Trust and respect:** Leaders must create an environment where they earn employee trust and respect and where employees are trusted and respected.	**Psychological safety:** Leaders must create an environment where there's no fear of recourse for speaking up or speaking your mind. Employees should feel accepted, and they should feel safe to not only speak up but to take risks.
Empowerment: Allow employees the freedom to do their jobs, enable them to take the right actions, and give them the authority to make decisions in their day-to-day roles.	**Wellness/well-being:** Healthy body, healthy mind. Encourage and support healthy lifestyles. Help employees dealing with mental health issues.	**Success:** Many employees aren't "just finding a job." Many are on a self-defined path to professional success. The first step is defining what that means and then working together to ensure that success happens.

Alignment: Employees aligned with the vision, mission, purpose, and values of the business will definitely have a better experience than those who aren't. Hire accordingly.

Those all sound soft and mushy, right? You might think that, but these are all essential and critical to the employee experience. And yet, employee experience isn't just about those things. When you see research about employee engagement and employee experience, the findings often include some of these items. But there's more.

Yes, employees want to be wrapped up in one nice big care package of employer love. But they have jobs to do. On top of being cared for, they need to be able to do great work. And when they can't do great work, they're not happy; customers feel it, and the business does too.

When I first start working with new clients, I interview the executive team, a sampling of employees across all departments, and a sampling of customers across various personas. Doing this allows me to get an unadulterated baseline of the current situation. My favorite conversations happen with employees because they call it as they see it. And quite often, what I hear is this: "We don't have the tools (or the processes are broken or the policies are outdated) to serve our customers the way they deserve to be served." Such a powerful statement—and such an affirmation of (1) what the employee experience is and (2) how the employee experience impacts the customer experience.

THE HARD STUFF

> Take the time to understand what keeps employees at your company; don't find out when it's too late.

On that note, what else is included in employee experience? In a nutshell, the rest of the story is all about tools, processes, policies, resources, workspace, and workplace (i.e., the hard stuff).

Tools: This seems simple enough, but you would be surprised at how many employees start with a new employer who don't have a computer or a desk on their first day (or within the first couple of weeks)! Tools include the desk, computer, software, printer, scanner, phone, vehicle, actual tools (e.g., a hammer), etc. Not every employee needs the same tools or the same types of tools (e.g., a graphic designer needs different hardware and software than an accounts payable person), but they've got to be well equipped from day one.

Processes: When there are no processes in place, employees make things up as they go. When there are broken processes, steps get missed, and things are done incorrectly. When there are old, outdated, and inefficient processes, those can be a waste of time. All of these lead to pain for employees and inconsistent experiences for customers.

Policies: If you've got outdated policies, policies that make employees' jobs harder than they should be, ambiguous or unclear policies, unfair policies, or any other policy issues, these are inhibitors keeping employees from doing their best work. Employees come to work wanting to do a good job; kill these bad or outdated policies.

Resources: Ensure that employees have the training, education, books, documentation, management support, teamwork, collaboration, etc. that they need to do their jobs well.

Workplace/workspace: Is there a quiet place for employees to work? Is it clean and roomy enough to get work done? Can calls and meetings be completed without distractions or background noise? How's the temperature and lighting? How's the parking situation? There's a lot to consider when it comes to the workplace and the employee's workspace; make it easy and painless for them.

Employees take pride in their work and are frustrated when they are inhibited from doing the jobs they were hired to do—and do them well. Some of the biggest pain points of their experiences are most often about their inability to do a good job. Unfortunately, they can't do a good job if they aren't provided with the tools, processes, policies, resources, and workspace needed to do just that.

In order for employees to do their jobs well and to ensure they have the tools, processes, policies, resources, and workspace needed to do just that, employee experience must be a primary focus for executives—and not just a focus but a reality too.

EMPLOYEE EXPERIENCE GAP

According to the Deloitte *2017 Global Human Capital Trends* report,[29] 80 percent of executives rated employee experience as very important, but only 22 percent said their companies excelled at designing and delivering the experience.

That's a big gap and a big problem. Why? There are a lot of reasons, including the following:

- **It's not a priority**: Instead, it's simply an annual engagement survey. You know by now that if you are going to survey an employee or a customer, you need to take action on what you learn!

- **No executive owner/ownership**: For customer experience, the C-suite executive is typically a chief customer officer. For many companies, there's no real equivalent for employee experience; the work isn't championed by—or hasn't been assigned to—anyone (in the C-suite). Roles such as people & culture officer or similar tell you that the organization has an employee champion.

- **Siloed HR departments**: They've traditionally been relegated to taking care of benefits and payroll, recruiting, hiring, etc.,

---

29 "Rewriting the rules for the digital age," Deloitte, accessed November 30, 2021, https://www2.deloitte.com/us/en/insights/focus/human-capital-trends/2017.html

and they can't seem to get resources to address an integration of those roles, all the actions and capabilities mentioned earlier, plus culture, and more.

- **Need updated listening tools and processes**: It's time to listen to employees in a variety of ways, not just that annual engagement survey. There must be pulse or transactional surveys, stay interviews, and other listening posts to understand and to engage with employees on an ongoing basis.

- **Disparate functions and disciplines**: The report states that HR tends to have a single focus or point-in-time engagement, as they call it, that has HR teams focusing on performance, diversity, wellness, workplace design, etc. as singular initiatives throughout the year rather than as an integrated discipline that must work together.

In the same report, 59 percent of respondents said they weren't ready to address the "employee experience challenge."

Clearly.

Two years later, Deloitte's 2019 report[30] showed that 84 percent of respondents rated the need to improve the employee experience as important, while only 28 percent identified it as one of the three most urgent issues facing their organization in 2019.

There is much work yet to be done.

WHY EMPLOYEE EXPERIENCE?

Similar to customer experience, executives often ask, "Why should we focus on the employee experience?" Some get it; many still don't. Let's start with some studies and statistics to show what is possible.

---

30   "2019 Global Human Capital Trends," Deloitte, accessed November 30, 2021, https://www2.deloitte.com/us/en/insights/focus/human-capital-trends/2019.html

A 2017 Massachusetts Institute of Technology (MIT) Center for Information Systems Research briefing[31] highlights MIT's research on employee experience. They found that companies in the top quartile of employee experience were twice as innovative, had double the customer satisfaction (reported via NPS), and had 25 percent higher profitability than those companies in the bottom quartile.

Jon Picoult of Watermark Consulting[32] did an analysis for employees, comparing the stock performance of employee experience leaders, or those who made *Fortune's* 100 Best Companies to Work For, versus the S&P 500 in general. Clearly, the results speak for themselves: the performance of *Fortune's* 100 Best Companies to Work For doubled that of the S&P 500.

Fortune[33] did their own study and compared these companies to the Russell 3000 index, and the returns were phenomenal. The Best Companies to Work For index saw returns that more than doubled the Russell 2000 index returns. In their research, *Fortune* noted that "it's the companies that employees say are great workplaces that demonstrate stronger financial performance, reduced turnover, and better customer and patient satisfaction than their peers."

Need more? Back in the early 1990s, when I was working at J.D. Power and Associates, W. Earl Sasser Jr. and Leonard Schlesinger (both from Harvard and two of the authors of "Putting the Service-Profit Chain to Work") came by our offices to talk about some of the things they were working on.

---

31   Kristine Dery and Ina M. Sebastian, "Building Business Value with Employee Experience," MIT, June 15, 2017, https://cisr.mit.edu/publication/2017_0601_EmployeeExperience_DerySebastian

32   "Why Watermark? Here's our Top Ten List," Watermark, accessed November 30, 2021, https://watermark-consult.net/about/why-watermark/#Loyalty-Lift

33   Catherine Yoshimoto and Ed Frauenheim, "The Best Companies to Work for Are Beating the Market," *Fortune*, February 27, 2018, https://fortune.com/2018/02/27/the-best-companies-to-work-for-are-beating-the-market/

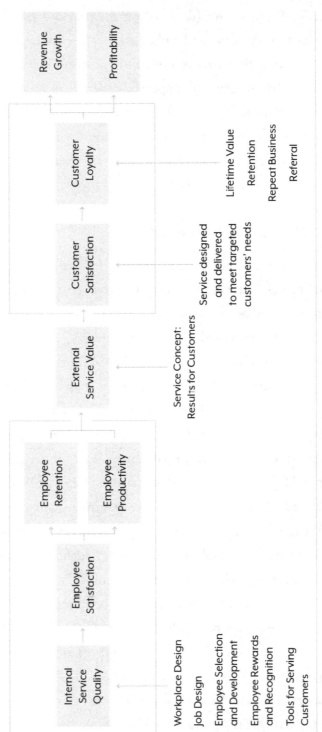

EXTERNAL

Target Market

INTERNAL

Operating Strategy and Service Delivery System

Revenue Growth

Profitability

Customer Loyalty

Lifetime Value

Retention

Repeat Business

Referral

Customer Satisfaction

Service designed and delivered to meet targeted customers' needs

External Service Value

Service Concept: Results for Customers

Employee Retention

Employee Productivity

Employee Satisfaction

Internal Service Quality

Workplace Design

Job Design

Employee Selection and Development

Employee Rewards and Recognition

Tools for Serving Customers

Source: Harvard Business Review, "Putting the Service-Profit Chain to Work,"
by James L. Heskett, Thomas O. Jones, Gary W. Loveman, W. Earl Sasser, Jr., and Leonard A. Schlesinger

The Service-Profit Chain (depicted on the previous page) resonated with us back in the day (and still does), but the concept really highlights the connection between what's happening inside the organization (i.e., the culture and employee experience) and what's being experienced outside by customers. I'm not just making up this connection; there's been a ton of work done over many years to show the correlation and to prove the point that the experience your employees have drives the experience your customers have.

REAL-WORLD EXAMPLES

It's great to write about the linkage, but let's talk about some real-world examples, some brands that put employees first and are reaping the outcomes and advantages noted above.

Delta Air Lines is well known for delivering great employee and customer experiences, thanks to their CEO, Ed Bastian. In February 2020, Delta announced a payout of more than $1 billion in profit sharing to employees to celebrate its accomplishments, "made possible by its employees around the world." Focusing on the employee experience is good for employees, for customers, and for the business.

Anne Mulcahy, former chairwoman and CEO of Xerox Corporation, has said, "Employees who believe that management is concerned about them as a whole person—not just as an employee—are more productive, more satisfied, more fulfilled. Satisfied employees mean satisfied customers, which leads to profitability."

Never underestimate the importance of leadership when it comes to the employee experience. Bob Chapman, CEO of Barry-Wehmiller, a phenomenal leader who knows the importance of caring for his employees, believes that when you create a workplace culture that truly values and cares for employees, the rest takes care of itself. He coined the term (and advocates for) "truly human leadership," which is a people-centric leadership style with the goal of ensuring team members feel valued, cared for, and an integral part of the company's purpose. His company just acquired its 101st business and since 1987 has experienced 18 percent compound revenue growth and 14 percent compound share price growth. While those numbers are impressive, Bob measures success by the way he and his leaders touch the lives of others. I have spoken with Bob several times, and I can tell you he's touched my life in an important way: give your time to others and care about others, and you will be forever blessed.

If you need another example of the impact of leadership and culture on the employee experience, look no further than WD-40 and CEO Garry Ridge, already introduced in an earlier chapter. In 2018, his employee satisfaction score sat at 92 percent, and he credits the success of the business to living the core values and building a culture of learning, which impacts the employee experience in so many ways. Under Garry's leadership, the business has grown from $300 million to more than $3 billion; take care of your people (employees and customers), and they will take care of the business.

And W.L. Gore, which has been named a Great Place to Work for twenty-one years in a row, has earned a spot on *Fortune*'s 100 Best Companies to Work For list every year since 1998. Their CEO, Jason Field, said: "We strive to ... unleash the natural curiosity and talent of our Associates to create products that improve lives." Eighty-nine percent of employees say that it's a great place to work. The bottom line: only 3 percent turnover.

Back in 2016, I interviewed Peter Aceto, then CEO of Tangerine Bank in Canada. We talked about the concept of *Weology*, also the title of his new book at the time. Weology is about building a culture where employees thrive, succeed, and are fulfilled, happy, and growing at work—a culture where every individual in the organization, regardless of who she is or what she does, has a voice (i.e., a culture where every individual matters). Sounds familiar? It reminds me now of Bob Chapman's concept of truly human leadership and of his book, *Everybody Matters: The Extraordinary Power of Caring for Your People Like Family*, which he coauthored with Raj Sisodia, founder and coauthor of *Conscious Capitalism*.

But I digress. Back to Weology. Why is this important? As Peter states in the book: "Being good to your own people is good business. When Me thrives, We benefit. Weology is about creating win-win scenarios. It's transparency without asterisks. It's a way of putting people first in the short term so that a company can thrive in the long term."

Bravo! Amen to that!

Peter is a student of Tony Hsieh and learned so much about building the right culture and focusing on your people from Tony. When I asked Peter about companies that had adopted this Weology approach, the one company he shared was pretty interesting, and it might shock you too! It was Guinness!

As he tells it, Guinness was a pioneer in prioritizing culture and the employee experience long before all of that was cool! Back in the early 1900s—more than a century ago! They had a gym and a swimming pool for their employees. You think today's Silicon Valley tech start-ups have perks? Guinness had a savings and loan division for staff, hospital and hospice stays were paid for, and employees received two-thirds of their salary if they were out sick. They received free medical and dental services and free prescriptions. Guinness paid above-market salaries and guaranteed lifetime employment. And much more.

But we know that culture and employee experience aren't about perks. Guinness was a pioneer in putting people first. And they had no reason to do it (i.e., they were already the largest brewery in the world), but they wanted employees to enjoy work and create better products. They wanted healthy, educated, and solvent employees working for them. When those things are taken care of, there's less stress on the employee, and she can be more productive. An important lesson, no doubt.

Even without the earlier graphic, you can see the linkage between culture, the employee experience, customer experience, and business outcomes. There is a clear linkage. Quite simply, without employees, you have no customer experience. It's time to make your employees a priority. *The* priority. And that's just good for business.

> Quite simply, without employees, you have no customer experience. It's time to make your employees a priority. **The** priority.

THE ROLE OF CULTURE FIT IN THE EMPLOYEE EXPERIENCE

I mentioned culture fit in an earlier chapter, and I could write an entire book on that topic alone. It's a controversial topic of late—revered by some, reviled by others—but I believe that's just because people don't truly understand what it means. **Culture fit simply means that employees believe in and align with the company's core values. I would also add that they are aligned with the mission, vision, and purpose.**

The controversy around culture fit arises in the fact that some believe that hiring for culture fit means everyone is the same, looks the same, and thinks the same, destroying things such as diversity, creativity, and innovation. On the contrary, it's a plus for employees and for the business. In the end, this culture alignment has everyone marching in the same direction, toward the same goals—but it doesn't mean they are all the same. You can have the most diverse, creative, and innovative group of employees when you hire for culture fit, and they will be aligned on "how we do things around here when no one is looking."

Once you've got your core values in place, the only way that hiring for culture fit can destroy diversity, creativity, and innovation is if they are not already widely accepted and encouraged in your organization. Hiring for culture fit does not mean that you'll only hire people with the same ideas or the same skin color. That's just ludicrous.

In determining the right people, the good-to-great companies placed greater weight on character attributes than on specific educational background, practical skills, specialized knowledge, or work experience.

—JIM COLLINS

Hiring for culture fit means you'll end up with a heterogeneous group of people with different experiences, education, thoughts, ideas, etc. but the same values, which I'm sure you surround yourself with in your personal life as well. If you can hang out with folks whose values aren't aligned with yours, you might want to reevaluate.

Culture fit is important from a couple of different angles: (1) the employee experience and (2) building the culture you desire. Remember, culture = core values + behaviors. Also important to remember is that culture is driven by the CEO and key executives. To build the culture you want, you have to do it deliberately, and that includes hiring people who will perpetuate that culture.

Clearly, some employees and potential employees already think about culture fit as they interview with companies. According to research by Robert Half,[34] "More than one-third of workers in the U.S. (35 percent) and Canada (40 percent) wouldn't accept a job that was a perfect match if the corporate culture clashed." On the flip side, "Nine out of 10 U.S. (91 percent) and Canadian (90 percent) managers said a candidate's fit with the organizational culture is equal to or more important than their skills and experience."

EMPLOYEES MORE FIRST

Tom Peters wrote years ago, referring to Hal Rosenbluth, CEO, Rosenbluth International: "Who comes first? Don't be silly, says King Hal; it's employees. That is—and this, dear Watson, is elementary—if you genuinely want to put customers first, you must put employees more first."

You've got to put employees more first. But in order to do that, the CEO must build and lead in a culture that was designed to put people first—before metrics, products, or profits. Remember that your corporate culture is a combination of what you create and what you allow. Executives must live it and reinforce it.

There's a lot of work to be done to design and deliver a great employee experience. That starts first with knowing what it is and what it entails. Now that you know, it's time to get started.

Let's shift gears and dive deeper into the concept of people first—before products, profits, and metrics.

---

34   "More than One-Third of Workers Would Pass on Perfect Job If Corporate Culture Was Not a Fit, Survey Finds," Robert Half, November 27, 2018, https://rh-us.mediaroom.com/2018-11-27-More-Than-One-Third-Of-Workers-Would-Pass-On-Perfect-Job-If-Corporate-Culture-Was-Not-A-Fit-Survey-Finds

DO YOU SEE ...	WHAT TO DO?	OUTCOMES OR BENEFITS
Employees are viewed as cogs in the wheel of leaders' and the business's success?	Talk to and get to know employees. Truly care about them. Rethink the connection between employees, customers, and business outcomes.	Be a great place to work. Employees want to work for you and want to give more. They refer their friends.
Employees are frustrated and turnover is high?	Evaluate the employee experience. Listen to employees. Conduct stay interviews. Fix the problems.	Employee productivity and retention increase.
Your HR team not hiring for culture fit?	Evaluate the current process. Bring values and culture questions into the interview process.	Alignment. Better employee experience. The desired culture.

CHAPTER 6

Principle 4—People before Products

Life's too short to build something nobody wants.

—ASH MAURYA

I recently attended a webinar about how to develop a customer-centric culture. Odd, no, since I'm writing the book on how to do that? Well, I'm always curious what others have to say on this topic. The webinar was solid, and the presenter did a good job of outlining many of the foundational elements she believed were needed to do just that. As webinars go, there was a Q&A segment at the end, and one of the questions asked was something along the lines of "But if I focus on the customer, won't that take away from my focus on the product?"

I had just taken a sip of my coffee, and I think it came out of my nose. I cleaned up the coffee and held my breath in hopes that the presenter would answer the question the way it should be answered. She did.

And yet, at the same time, I'm shocked that someone would ask that question. (OK, only mildly shocked, given the challenges that we customer experience professionals have, but just pretend I was shocked. It makes for a better story.)

Here's the real question: isn't it all the same stuff?

Money is being spent by businesses every day to develop and build products, and yet they don't factor in the needs and perspectives of the customer? How does that work?

Listen. It's all about putting the customer at the heart of all you do. It's all about the customer. It's why you're in business—for and about the customer. If you're designing a product without thinking about the customer—without understanding her needs, her pain points, her problems to solve, and her jobs to be done—forget it. The product will die. Maybe not tomorrow but it will die eventually.

In a world where products and services are becoming more and more commoditized, customer experience is the only true differentiator. That means that brands need to fight to stay relevant—yet they truly struggle to not get "Blockbuster'd."[35]

It's all about putting the customer at the heart of all you do.

Jim Keyes, CEO of Blockbuster, stated in 2008 in a Motley Fool interview:[36] "Neither Redbox nor Netflix are even on the radar screen in terms of competition." He was more focused on Walmart and Apple and laughed in the face of the disruption that was happening in his own industry. Blockbuster filed for bankruptcy in 2010. Today, Netflix is worth $230 billion, although they are in the midst of their own competitive struggles at the moment with the onslaught of many new streaming services.

---

35   "Ouch: Getting Blockbuster'd," CB Insights, August 22, 2017, https://www.cbinsights.com/research/ouch-getting-blockbusterd/

36   Rick Munarriz, "Blockbuster CEO Has Answers," The Motley Fool, updated April 5, 2017, https://www.fool.com/investing/general/2008/12/10/blockbuster-ceo-has-answers.aspx

Jonathan Salem Baskin,[37] a former Blockbuster executive, wrote in *Forbes* that Blockbuster was trying to reimagine itself as a convenience store. Clearly not a sound strategy or one that its customers were aligned with. He wrote:

"The problem with this strategy is that it never acknowledged, let alone addressed, the fundamental promise and peril of the business: If people didn't come to find movies they wish they hadn't missed in the theaters, no amount of add-on retailing could replace that once-glorious rental income. Blockbuster didn't have a technology problem—digital distribution was minimal, albeit talked about incessantly—but rather a customer problem. It gave them no reason to visit stores in lieu of a latest, greatest hit."

There are plenty of examples of companies not putting the "customer" in *customer* experience. If you make decisions, define strategies, develop products or services, design websites, etc., and you don't include the customer and her voice in any of that work, you will fail. Customers have choices. They will go elsewhere. They will buy from companies who find products for them. They prefer that over companies who find customers for their products.

Don't find customers for your products; find products for your customers.

—SETH GODIN

---

37   Jonathan Salem Baskin, "The Internet Didn't Kill Blockbuster, the Company Did It to Itself," *Forbes*, November 8, 2013, https://www.forbes.com/sites/jonathansalembaskin/2013/11/08/ the-internet-didnt-kill-blockbuster-the-company-did-it-to-itself/#4833e7636488

EMPATHY AND HUMAN-CENTERED DESIGN

Doug Dietz was in tears as he relayed the story[38] of a huge mistake he made when he designed the MRI machine for GE Healthcare. He was so proud of the machine he had designed, and when he had the opportunity to see it installed in a hospital, he jumped at the chance, even telling the technician that the machine was up for an International Design Excellence Award.

After the installation, he stayed to observe patients as they entered the room and prepared for their scans. The first patient was a little girl who was crying, anxious and scared about what she was about to go through. The technician called an anesthesiologist to sedate the girl so that she could get through the procedure. It was then that Doug learned that about 80 percent of kids coming in for MRIs had to be sedated. If no anesthesiologist was available, the scan had to be postponed, causing stress for the parents and child and backlogs for the hospital. Not an efficient process for anyone, for sure.

Doug's mistake? He forgot about the customer when he designed the machine. He didn't design it from the customer's perspective, certainly not from a child's perspective. This tore at his soul. How could he create such fear and anxiety for the kids? He went home and did some soul-searching and some research and learned about a human-centered design course being offered at the Stanford d.school. After completing the weeklong course, he flew home and resolved to redesign the MRI experience using what he'd just learned.

He spent time observing and talking to kids, learning what they enjoyed doing, what made them happy, and what made them feel safe.

---

38   Doug Dietz, "The Design Thinking Journey: Using Empathy to Turn Tragedy into Triumph," filmed at TEDxStGeorgesSchoolMiddletown, Middletown, RI, September 24, 2017, https://www.ted.com/talks/doug_dietz_the_design_thinking_journey_using_empathy_to_turn_tragedy_into_triumph

In the end, he didn't redesign the machine but the room in which the machine resides. The rooms were designed to look like a campground, a pirate ship, the circus, a jungle, a spaceship, etc. And each different design of his Adventure Series came with a script, the story that the technician could tell the kids as they went on this adventure. They had to "walk the plank" to get onto the pirate ship, listen for the boom as the spaceship shifted into hyperdrive, lie perfectly still and watch the goldfish jump over them, dig through the pirate's chest for treasures after the procedure, and more.

The result? When he shared his story in a TED Talk in 2012, it had been about eighteen months since the initial installations. Only *two* kids had to be sedated during that time. Patient satisfaction had increased 90 percent. Cancellations and backlogs were eradicated. And kids were saying, "Mom, Dad, can we come back again tomorrow?"

Operational efficiencies were introduced, and as a result, patient volume went up because they were able to move more patients through in a day. That equates to more money for the hospital. And in the end, it was a financial win for GE Healthcare as well.

Doug's story shows that putting the customer at the center of what you do, at the center of designing your products, definitely leads to innovation. When you start problem-solving with empathy for your customers, innovation is a natural outcome.

People before products. Start with the people. Start with empathy. Put the customer into the customer experience. Don't allow the customer to be an afterthought.

Empathy is about standing in someone else's shoes, feeling with his or her heart, seeing with his or her eyes. Not only is empathy hard to outsource and automate, but it makes the world a better place.

—DANIEL PINK

SOLVING CUSTOMER PROBLEMS

I love this classic example of making sure you think about your customers as you develop your products. This one dates back to 1876 when Henry Heinz[39] needed to solve some problems with what was then loosely known and referred to as "ketchup." He didn't invent ketchup; he just did it better than others.

What problems did he solve? A couple. First, he knew people didn't have the time to create labor-intensive sauces and preserves, so his product would save people time, and there's huge value in that for customers. Second, he knew that customers were looking for safe, reliable, healthy, and flavorful ketchup because existing ketchup products were not. They were created from oysters (yes!), celery, mushrooms, and a bunch of other vegetables, just not tomatoes. They weren't healthy, and they certainly weren't flavorful. As a matter of fact, his competition was putting their products into barrels, stone crocks, and brown or green glass bottles to disguise what they were selling; the products were basically sludge, often rotten or spoiled.

Heinz, on the other hand, put the customer first and wanted to make sure customers could see what they were getting. He wanted to (1) reassure them that they were buying pure, hygienic, and healthy products and (2) distinguish his products from less healthy and less flavorful products. He was so focused on delivering value and a pure product that he would even buy back products that didn't look good or outlived shelf life. He used clear glass bottles for his ketchup, which was basically unheard of. No one else was doing that. It's what Heinz became known for: having the best, cleanest, and healthiest product.

---

39   "The Food that Built America," The History Channel, accessed November 30, 2021, https://www.history.com/shows/the-food-that-built-america

Ah, yes. Those glass bottles. They were all about the customer at the time, but they, too, became a problem for customers. One problem was solved, and eventually, another was created. There's even a commercial about that bottle. They played up the wait. They said the flavor was so good that it was worth the wait. But how long did you wait—how hard did you try—to get ketchup out of that bottle? Your earworm for today is "Anticipation. It's Making Me Wait." Google the commercial! So it only took 113 years to fix *that* problem, and now we have the squeeze bottle for ketchup.

CROWDSOURCING YOUR PRODUCT DESIGN

A few years back, Hasbro crowdsourced their next Monopoly character on Facebook by asking people to vote on which character would become the next game piece. In the end, the iron game piece got the boot, and the cat was voted in, bringing pet lovers to parity; dog lovers already had their game piece.

So what did listening to customers do for them? Did it pay in the end? According to a *USA Today* article,[40] Hasbro saw revenue growth in their games category and called the Monopoly character contest "tremendously successful." Subsequently, they crowdsourced other changes to Monopoly, along with changes to other games. Is this the sole reason for their revenue growth? Only they know. But what I do know is that it's a great way to (1) listen to the wants, needs, and preferences of your customers and (2) engage your customers.

By the way, Hasbro is not the only brand to crowdsource product ideas. Starbucks, Ben and Jerry's, LAY'S, and others have all used crowdsourcing to listen to customers and to generate new product

---

40   "Monopoly Cat Token Contest Lifts Hasbro Sales," *USA Today*, April 22, 2013, https://www.usatoday.com/story/money/business/2013/04/22/hasbro-monopoly-contest-lifts-sales/2103069/

ideas. The "involve them in the change" mantra applies not only to organizational change but also to product change.

> *This may seem simple, but you need to give customers what they want, not what you think they want. And, if you do this, people will keep coming back.*

—JOHN ILHAN, CRAZY JOHN'S

ENDLESS TENACITY FOR CUSTOMERS

I was recently introduced to Sendbird, an in-app chat and messaging application programming interface used by a variety of brands that you're familiar with, including DoorDash, Yelp, Reddit, Teledoc, Hinge, and more. One of the things that struck me about this brand is their first core value, endless tenacity for customers.

You can find a description of this core value on their site. It reads:

Our origin story begins with the customer. Customers existed before businesses. They faced a problem for which few people dared to find a solution, and created customer value. Businesses we know today evolved from the organized and deliberate effort to find solutions to these problems. We exist, first, to satisfy customers. And then to leap beyond the status quo and create innovative solutions to problems that customers may not even be aware of yet. This leap might be challenging and frustrating, but endless tenacity is the true springboard to customer happiness.

On his *Positive Tenacity* channel[41] on YouTube, Sendbird CEO John Kim says, "The more understanding you have about your customers—who they are, what problems they are trying to solve,

---

41   "SaaS/B2B: How to Get Your First 100 Customers," Positive Tenacity, uploaded January 11, 2020, https://www.youtube.com/watch?v=c48Y0O_qqDI

what keeps them up at night—the easier it is to build your product and scale your company."

Amen to that!

This is what I'm talking about when I say people before products. You've got to understand your customers and develop products that help them solve problems and give them peace of mind. Doing otherwise is foolish and painful. It might even (eventually) be fateful, like the Blockbuster story.

I've been a start-up advisor to several tech companies, but I'm also frequently contacted by tech start-ups because they want to show me their products, pick my brain, and get my thoughts about their products, business model, etc. It always amazes me when I ask them this question: What problem are you solving for your customers? They can't answer the question. They haven't done the research. If you're a start-up, do the research. Talk to potential customers. Understand how you can help them improve their lives or solve some problem. It sounds like a lot of work, and maybe you feel like it distracts you or takes too much time. But trust me. You will not regret taking the time to do that.

Customer understanding is critical to success, to your ability to put people before products. I will cover this in detail in chapter 9.

When in doubt, talk to customers.

—JOHN KIM, CEO OF SENDBIRD

DO YOU SEE ...	WHAT TO DO?	OUTCOMES OR BENEFITS
Product designers focusing on the product, not on customers?	Have them talk to customers. They need to get to know who's going to use the product. Have the CX team share customer feedback and data with them.	Products that solve problems for customers.
We build products because we have great ideas.	Talk to customers. Understand the problems to solve. Incorporate learnings into product design and development.	Products that solve problems for customers.
We don't do customer research. We work on gut instinct.	Stop. Talk to customers. Do the work to understand customers and the problems they are trying to solve.	Products that solve problems for customers.

CHAPTER 7

Principle 5—People before Profits

Money is never a purpose. Money is always a result.

—SIMON SINEK

OK. Reserve judgment on this chapter until you read it. You may think I'm nuts with a title like that, but when I say "people before profits," I don't mean that profits aren't important. A business obviously needs to make money to survive. But I'm immediately taken to that outdated management theory that "companies are in business to maximize shareholder value." The purpose of a business is to create and to nurture customers. Hat tip to Peter Drucker on that one.

Check out this quote: "I think it is a moral requirement to make money when you can ... to sell the product for the highest price."

That's an actual quote from an actual CEO.[42] As a matter of fact, it's a quote from Nirmal Mulye, CEO of Nostrum Laboratories. He's defending his decision to raise the price of a drug fivefold to $2,400! Nostrum Laboratories makes the generic version of a urinary tract infection antibiotic (nitrofurantoin), which had sold for $474.75 until

---

42   David Crow, "Pharma Chief Defends 400% Drug Price Rise as a Moral Requirement," *Financial Times*, September 11, 2018, https://www.ft.com/content/48b0ce2c-b544-11e8-bbc3-ccd7de085ffe

the price of the brand-name version (by Casper Pharma) of the drug rose to $2,800.

Mulye's response: "The brand hiked the price. We are just trying to bring a cheaper alternative to the brand. So I'm the savior, not the villain, and everyone is making me the villain." Then he added: "This is a capitalist economy, and if you can't make money, you can't stay in business. We have to make money when we can."

He said that he is "in this business to make money." Clearly.

But what about the customer? And the impact on the customer and her health?

Contrast that with George Merck,[43] cofounder of Merck, who gave a speech in 1950 at the Medical College of Virginia at Richmond in which he shook up the pharmaceutical industry by saying: "We try to remember that medicine is for the patient. We try never to forget that medicine is for the people. It is not for the profits. The profits follow, and if we have remembered that, they have never failed to appear." According to the Merck website, this philosophy is still very much alive and embraced by both leaders and employees today.

In our quest to invent medicines and vaccines that save and improve lives, the core of who we are is embodied in our values and standards. They are fundamental to our success—now and into the future.

—KEN FRAZIER, EXECUTIVE CHAIRMAN
OF THE BOARD, MERCK

---

43   "Our History," Merck, accessed December 1, 2021, https://www.merck.com/company-overview/history/

MEANS VERSUS OUTCOMES

While creating and maximizing shareholder value is important to any public company, it is an outcome, not a means. There are means to achieving that outcome, and they include putting employees and customers first, ahead of profits. Companies succeed if and when:

- employees want to work for them,
- customers want to—and actually do—buy their products,
- vendors and suppliers want to partner with them,
- people want them to locate in—and be a part of—their communities, and
- shareholders buy their stocks.

Companies have more constituents than shareholders and more responsibilities than delivering value to just shareholders. The rest of their constituents must receive value as well. Put employees more first, then customers, and watch the business thrive.

DO YOU PUT PROFITS BEFORE PEOPLE?

I've seen a particular phenomenon many times: executives decide to put their employee experience and customer experience improvement efforts on pause because sales figures are down for the quarter. Clearly, the blame is that the people focus has derailed them from business development and closing deals; there can be no other reason for this (she said with all the sarcasm in the world).

> **Putting people front and center in your business is critical to success.**

Putting people front and center in your business is critical to success. Unfortunately, the immediate, short-term pressures of the business often drive out long-term goals and objectives.

Too many executives today still live by the old management adage, "companies are in business to maximize shareholder value." In doing so, they put profits before people, rather than the other way around. Ironically, in the 1970s, Jack Welch was a huge proponent of that adage, but within the last fifteen years or so, he has renounced it, calling it "the dumbest idea in the world" and saying:

> *Shareholder value is a result, not a strategy. Your main constituencies are your employees, your customers, and your products. Managers and investors should not set share price increases as their overarching goal. Short-term profits should be allied with an increase in the long-term value of a company.*

—JACK WELCH

When companies (executives) put profits before people, they are driven by:

- short-term thinking;
- shortsightedness;
- impatience;
- money, metrics, margins, numbers, and revenue; and
- shareholders.

These are the things that cause executives to stop improvement efforts, to stop putting the focus on the defining principles in this book, and shift focus and resources solely on closing deals and making the numbers. Nothing else matters.

When in reality, focusing on the employee and on the customer first are all about ensuring you can close deals and make your numbers. Focus on the former, and the latter follows.

Peter Drucker says that the purpose of a business is to create a customer. You can't create a customer if you don't have the right people in place to deliver value to the customer, if you don't understand who the customer is and what her needs are, and if you're not designing and creating products that help her solve problems or get jobs done.

Seth Godin wrote:[44]

> So how do companies do that? How do they drive up value for employees so that they can deliver value for customers—and, ultimately, for the business?

The purpose of a company is to serve its customers.

Its obligation is to not harm everyone else.

And its opportunity is to enrich the lives of its employees.

Somewhere along the way, people got the idea that maximizing investor return was the point. It shouldn't be. That's not what democracies ought to seek in chartering corporations to participate in our society.

The great corporations of a generation ago, the ones that built key elements of our culture, were run by individuals who had more on their mind than driving the value of their options up.

So how do companies do that? How do they drive up value for employees so that they can deliver value for customers—and, ultimately, for the business?

---

44   Seth Godin, "What Are Corporations For?," Seth's Blog, October 18, 2015, https://seths.blog/2015/10/what-are-corporations-for/

- Create a culture where people are first.
- Define and socialize your values.
- Hire the right people, particularly those who fit your culture.
- Take care of employees, and they will take care of customers. Don't just treat employees as cogs in the wheel. Trust, motivate, reward, and respect them.
- Let employees know how their work matters and how it impacts the business. Be open to ideas and suggestions from employees, and use them.
- Listen to employees, learn from what you hear, and do something with the feedback. They want the business to succeed as much as you do. Value their input, and show them that you care by using it to make changes and improvements.
- Invest in your employees. Coach, train, and develop them, and ensure they are on a path to career success.
- Treat people like people. See human. Be human.
- Create a workplace where policies and processes don't hinder an employee's ability to do his job—and do it well. Or hinder his ability to deliver a great experience to his customers.
- Live a life of servant leadership. Put the needs and interests of your people before your own. Take care of your people.
- Leaders must communicate, and be open and transparent. Develop a culture of transparency.

I'll say it again: it's a mindset shift and then a behavior shift. I can tell you all of those things have to happen, but you must lead and run the business differently. It begins with you.

Your employees come first. And if you treat your employees right, guess what? Your customers come back, and that makes your shareholders happy. Start with employees and the rest follows from that.

—HERB KELLEHER

Unfortunately, in most organizations, the culture looks like the pyramid in this image below, where mission, vision, and values might frame the foundation for the culture, but revenue and profits take priority over employees and customers—and drive everything that's being done in the organization. These companies live by the "we're in business to maximize shareholder value" mantra.

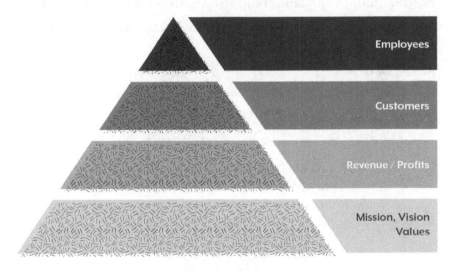

TYPICAL ORGANIZATIONAL CULTURE
© 2017 | CX Journey Inc.

Contrast that with a people-centric culture (image on the next page), where, without a shadow of a doubt, the company foundation is its mission, vision, values, and purpose. These companies have a strong culture and use these foundational elements day in and day out to operate the business. Once the company is grounded in a well-defined and clearly communicated mission, vision, values, and purpose, they've got a solid basis for a people-focused and people-centric culture. By the way, the corporate vision must be aligned with the customer experience vision. They might actually be one and the same. This applies to your corporate mission and customer experience mission, too—aligned and potentially the same statements.

Next, you'll see that I've reordered the layers of the typical organization culture pyramid and have added a new layer that is all about the executives and executive alignment. As I mentioned in chapter 4, if your executive team is not aligned with the business goals and outcomes, both internal and external, then neither is the rest of the organization. In the same vein, if executives don't embrace servant leadership, then it will be difficult to foster that people-centric culture.

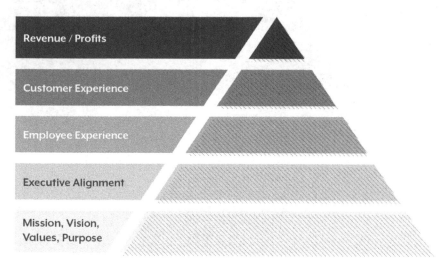

PEOPLE-CENTRIC CULTURE
© 2017 | CX Journey Inc.

The next layer in the pyramid is your employees, who will benefit from a company built on a solid mission, vision, values, and purpose—all of which become not only the basis for hiring, firing, and promoting but also the basis for executive behavior and decision-making. And they benefit from an executive team that is aligned and working together.

As you now know, employees must come more first. The employee experience drives the customer experience. When you've got happy, engaged, satisfied, and empowered employees, customers benefit in their experience. And so, the customer experience is the next layer of the pyramid.

And when you focus on the people—employees and customers—first, then the numbers—revenue/profits—will come.

Invest in your employees, and your business will thrive.

—DAN PRICE, GRAVITY PAYMENTS

Dan Price, founder and CEO of Gravity Payments, has proven that. He's the CEO who elevated the minimum wage for all of his employees to $70,000 per year. He prided himself on caring for his people and treating them well, but when he was gut punched by an employee who told him that his $35,000 annual salary left him feeling ripped off, Price took that conversation to heart (literally) and decided to fix things. It's a great story, and if you haven't heard of it, you've likely been asleep under a rock for the last ten years. Not only did he raise annual employee wages, he also cut his own from $1.1 million to $70,000.

The employee experience drives the customer experience.

Was it worth it? Well, revenues doubled their previous rates, profits rose as much as they had the previous year before he instituted this plan, and productivity increased by 30 to 40 percent. Both customer and employee retention numbers were unheard of. You decide.

ANTI-CEO PLAYBOOK

Putting employees and customers before revenue and profits means that your executives are making decisions with their employees and customers in mind at all times. They are doing what's best for employees and, ultimately, for customers so that, in the end, the business benefits.

> *Today's business book says: business exists to maximize profit for the shareholders. I think that's the dumbest idea I've ever heard in my life.*

—HAMDI ULUKAYA, CEO OF CHOBANI

(Clearly, he and Jack Welch are on the same page.)

If there's any doubt that that is possible, look no further than Hamdi Ulukaya,[45] CEO of Chobani. In January 2005, he received a flyer in the mail advertising a fully equipped yogurt plant for sale in Upstate New York. It was an eighty-five-year-old plant that was being closed by Kraft Foods, and he wanted to go see it. The factory was rundown and smelled like sour milk, but the thing that hit him hardest was the employees—all fifty-five of them—silent and heartbroken as they tore down the plant. They had given the business their lives, and now the business was giving up on them.

The people were the reason Hamdi ended up buying the plant. And their (former) CEO was the reason he put together the "Anti-CEO Playbook" as he pondered:

---

45   Hamdi Ulukaya, "The Anti-CEO Playbook," TED2019, accessed December 1, 2021, https://www.ted.com/talks/hamdi_ulukaya_the_anti_ceo_playbook/transcript?

"I just kept wondering: What is this all about? Corporate America says it's about profits. Mainstream business says it's about money. The CEO playbook says it's about shareholders. And so much is sacrificed for it—its factories, communities, jobs. But not by CEOs. CEOs have their employees suffer for them. But yet, the CEO's pay goes up and up and up. And so many people are left behind."

What does the "Anti-CEO Playbook" entail? It's built upon four constructs.

1. *Gratitude*: Take care of your employees first.
2. *Community*: Ask how the business can help the community, not what the community can do for the business, e.g., tax breaks.
3. *Responsibility*: Business, not government, is in the best position to make a change in today's world.
4. *Accountability*: The CEO shouldn't report to the board but to consumers.

As Hamdi explains it:

"The new way of business—it's the consumer we report to, not to the corporate boards. You see, if you are right with your people, if you are right with your community, if you are right with your product, you will be more profitable, you will be more innovative, you will have more passionate people working for you and a community that supports you. And that's what the Anti-CEO Playbook is all about."

Chobani is the top-selling strained yogurt brand in the US. You can't really argue with that. He's doing something right. Focus on the people, and the numbers will come.

Great leaders are willing to sacrifice the numbers to save the people. Poor leaders sacrifice the people to save the numbers.

—SIMON SINEK

TRULY HUMAN LEADERSHIP

I was first introduced to Bob Chapman, CEO of Barry-Wehmiller, back in 2012. I had listened to his TEDx Talk and written about it on my blog. He reached out to me and asked if we could talk. Of course, I was delighted because his message resonated with me, and I was excited to hear more. At the time, he shared with me that he and Simon Sinek had met and had talked about starting a leadership institute, which they did. (I even attended a course back in 2019.) In 2018, I reached out to Bob about a dilemma I was having with a client, and he took the time to guide me on how to approach the situation. He practices what he preaches, truly.

Bob and Raj Sisodia wrote *Everybody Matters*, in which they outline his approach to leadership that I mentioned earlier, something he calls "truly human leadership," which is about measuring success by the way you touch the lives of your people. If you want a great story about putting people before profit, look no further than Bob. In an *Industry Week* interview,[46] he said:

"Business has always been about product and profit; it's never been about people. We say it's about people, purpose, and performance. It starts with the fundamental responsibility for the lives of the people that we have the privilege of inviting into our company, organized around a purpose that inspires them to share their gifts fully [and that] creates value for all stakeholders to sustain us."

And it works! Barry-Wehmiller has seen annual growth of about 18 percent for the last twenty-five years. Businesses that put people

---

46   Patricia Panchak, "A New Path to Business and Operational Excellence," *Industry Week*, April 12, 2016, https://www.industryweek.com/leadership/companies-executives/article/21972348/a-new-path-to-business-and-operational-excellence

and purpose before profit see returns that outperform average stock market returns.

DO YOU SEE ...	WHAT TO DO?	OUTCOMES OR BENEFITS
The "typical organizational culture" pyramid describes my business.	Time to flip the script, execute on what you're learning in this book, and put people before profits.	Outcomes ($$) are real.
We believe the purpose of a business is to maximize shareholder value.	Time to build the business case that shows that employees drive value for customers, which creates value for the business.	Outcomes ($$) are real.
Shortsighted leaders who struggle with short-term thinking?	Talk to employees and customers. Listen to their pains. Solve for them.	Outcomes ($$) are real.

CHAPTER 8

Principle 6—People before Metrics

*So valuable is the human element that I will not let this Company lose
the human touch which has been largely responsible for its success.*

—D. L. B. SMITH, FOUNDER, SELECTIVE INSURANCE

Several years ago, I was reading an article about an interview[47] with
then new Anaheim Angels player Albert Pujols. His comments really
struck a chord and were a great reminder of what all too many who
measure employee and customer satisfaction end up doing: ***focusing
on the score.***

In the interview, Albert was asked: "In 2011, you just missed
getting 100 RBIs and a .300 average. What is your philosophy about
personal statistics in relation to goals?"

His response:

"I don't get caught up in numbers. I think when you start doing
that, you start disrespecting the game. You start forgetting what your
main focus is, and that's winning and helping your ball club to win.
Last year was the best year because we were the world champions. At
the end of the season, you're going to have plenty of time to look at

---

47   Annette Franz, "Baseball Stats and CX Metrics (No, It's Not a Moneyball Story!)," CX Journey, July 10, 2012,
      https://cx-journey.com/2012/07/baseball-stats-and-cx-metrics-no-its.html

your numbers. I think the main thing that I pray about every day is to stay healthy and then go from there."

I couldn't have summed it up any better had I planted the question with Albert myself! Let's break it down and draw out the lessons from his comments:

1. **Don't get caught up in the numbers.** If you're tracking customer experience metrics, great. But capture feedback, and focus on improving the experience, not the score. Analyze and operationalize the voice of the customer, and improve processes, products, services, etc. The score can rally the troops around the right thing, but the score shouldn't be the primary focus.

2. **When you focus on the score, you disrespect the game.** Absolutely! When you focus on your chosen metric and how to move the needle, your focus is misplaced. (And what if you're tracking the wrong metric? What if it's one that doesn't matter to, or correlate with, the customer experience?) You are likely doing tactical things to move the needle, but you're not looking at the big picture or thinking strategically to improve the overall experience ... and, ultimately, to grow your business.

3. **You forget your main focus.** You forget that it's *not* about the score; it's about giving it your best to win the game. It's about using that voice of the customer to deliver a superior customer experience—one that has been designed from the customer's viewpoint. It's about building a culture that facilitates and enhances the experience for both employees and customers. Remember that when you take care of your people, they will take care of your customers, and the business will win.

Two sidebar baseball lessons that I'll throw in here …

4. **If you build it, they will come.** I couldn't resist throwing in this reference. (*Field of Dreams*, right?) If you build a customer-centric culture and a brand with a purpose, then other like-minded individuals (employees and customers) will want to become a part of that culture. And that leads us to …

5. **Raving fans.** What's a baseball team without its raving fans? What's a business without its raving fans—both employees and customers?

OK, back to Albert and his response …

6. **Plenty of time to look at the numbers.** Albert is right. You can look at the numbers at some point because they'll be an indicator for you as to how well the business is doing, but if you look at the numbers every day, it will just drive you nuts. If you track the metrics daily, you're not thinking strategically about the game and what it takes to win. You're only thinking about how you can move the numbers tomorrow. Don't be shortsighted!

7. **Stay healthy, and go from there.** The difference between expectations and performance leads to satisfaction (or dissatisfaction). Identify customer needs and expectations, and work to not only meet them but to exceed them, regularly. Transform your culture into one that is healthy, one that puts the customer's viewpoint at the center of every decision.

Albert had a rough start to that season, despite joining the Angels that year with an impressive home run history and an out-of-this-world contract. Expectations ran high, and he fumbled (yeah, I know, mixing my sports) out of the gate. Was he focusing on the numbers? Everyone else around him (media and fans) certainly was. He finally got his footing, and once he hit that first home run, he started doing so regularly. Perhaps he settled in, forgot about focusing on his numbers, and started to play the game. Lesson learned.

GOODHART'S LAW

Have you ever heard of Goodhart's Law? It states: "When a measure becomes a target, it ceases to be a good measure." Or similarly, "Any observed statistical regularity will tend to collapse once pressure is placed upon it for control purposes."

According to Wikipedia,[48] its origin lies in finance and economics:

The original formulation by Goodhart, a former advisor to the Bank of England and Emeritus Professor at the London School of Economics, is this: "As soon as the government attempts to regulate any particular set of financial assets, these become unreliable as indicators of economic trends." This is because investors try to anticipate what the effect of the regulation will be and invest so as to benefit from it.

Another example that's been cited frequently is this one about a nail factory in Russia.

The goal of central planners was to measure performance of the factories, so factory operators were given targets around the number of nails produced. To meet and exceed the targets, factory operators produced millions of tiny, useless nails. When targets were switched to the total weight of nails produced, operators instead produced several enormous, heavy, and useless nails.

Are you making useless nails or achieving your desired outcomes—for all constituents? This is what happens at many companies when it

---

48   "Goodhart's Law," Wikipedia, accessed December 1, 2021, https://en.wikipedia.org/wiki/Goodhart%27s_law

comes to customer experience (or other) metrics. The target, not the customer and her desired outcome, becomes the focus. Moving the needle is what it's all about, at all costs.

This law is a big problem, and quite honestly, it's also somewhat of a root cause behind inaction and your inability to change. Companies focus on the metric, on moving the metric, and not on the customer and the customer experience. Listening to customers becomes all about "*How do we rate today?*" And while it's good to gauge your performance, the movement of the metric is an

> **Are you making useless nails or achieving your desired outcomes— for all constituents?**

outcome down the line—the first area of focus ought to be, What's going on with the customer experience, and how do you improve it?

But instead, too many executive conversations start with "*How do we improve the metric?*" rather than "*How do we improve the experience?*"

A metric is just that, a metric, a way of measuring your progress. If you make it the end point, you'll fail at the journey.

CUSTOMER EXPERIENCE GAP

Let me jump out of the sports world and bring things back to business (not that sports isn't a business). There's this thing called the **customer experience perception gap**; it was uncovered by Bain back in 2005,[49] although they referred to it as a "delivery gap." Their findings were as follows:

---

49   James Allen et al., "Closing the Delivery Gap," Bain, September 27, 2005, https://www.bain.com/insights/closing-the-delivery-gap/

Eighty percent of executives believe that they are delivering a superior customer experience, while only 8 percent of customers agree.

Wow! These executives are so off base (sorry, baseball again) on their perceptions or understandings of their customers and the experience! How is that even possible? Why do they think this way? It's certainly not because business leaders fail to recognize the importance of their customers. Well, at least they give customers lip service: *more than 95 percent of management teams Bain surveyed claim to be customer focused.*

Why does the gap exist? Bain cited two key reasons, which I'll put into my own thoughts and words.

1. *Imbalance between acquisition and retention*: Executives focus disproportionately on acquisition over retention, thereby misdirecting their attention away from their current customer base. They focus on growth. CEOs find growth sexy, and that's OK, but not all growth comes from new customers. And acquiring new customers costs 5–25 times more than retaining existing customers. Doesn't matter. The conversation goes like this: "Hey! We acquired ten thousand new customers last month! We must be doing something right! Must have a great experience!" But they never talk about the thousands who left at the same time (a.k.a. the leaky bucket syndrome). (I know this for a fact. I've had clients who have shared this secret with me.)

   When businesses focus on acquisition over retention, they do whatever it takes to bring those new customers in the door: freebies, promotions, discounts, free shipping, coupon scams that make customers think they are getting a deal, etc. And that gets expensive. Doing what you need to do to keep customers is different from what it takes to move the number, to increase acquisition and growth metrics.

Just because you've got customers pouring in the door doesn't mean that you have a great experience, especially if you can't keep those customers. When businesses focus on acquisition over retention, they do different things, and they do things differently than if they focused on retention more than acquisition—or at the very least, had more balance between the two.

2. *Lopsided focus on moving the needle on metrics*: Companies also focus more on "collecting data" and tracking metrics (NPS, consumer satisfaction score, customer lifetime value, etc.) than on analyzing the data, socializing it, and using it to improve the experience. If you've ever received a candy bar, a (large) discount off your next purchase, a free oil change, or a free Sam's Club membership (I've been offered all of these and more) with a plea to *"Please rate me a 10 out of 10 on the survey you'll get tomorrow, otherwise I'll get fired"* (not get my commission, not get promoted, etc.), then you know that business is focused on the metric and not on the customer and the customer experience—or the employees, for that matter.

    Car dealerships have always been the worst offenders of this. All that these businesses want to do is move the needle. It's bad behavior for the business, it's icky for the customer, and it's not that great for the employee, either, because most likely she's comped on the score and is begging for her bonus.

    When businesses focus on the metric, they do whatever it takes to move the needle, which means they do different things and they do things differently than if they focused on improving the experience, which would ultimately move the needle and benefit everyone.

DOES THE BAIN RESEARCH STILL HOLD?

So that particular Bain research was from 2005. Sadly, the numbers haven't moved all that much since then. Why is that? What do you think that's a result of?

In 2019, CX Network released a report on the state of customer experience.[50] They asked customer experience practitioners what the biggest stumbling blocks are for them when they want to increase their customer-centricity and keep up with constantly rising customer expectations. The number one response was "competing priorities."

You have "competing priorities"? What does that mean? What are those competing priorities? What could possibly compete with the foundation or the purpose of your business? What business initiative could you be considering that doesn't impact the customer?

In 2018, Capgemini[51] released a report that had slightly better findings, which means companies had only made *some* progress in the thirteen years since Bain's report. Their findings still showed a disconnect between customer expectations and companies' beliefs. Capgemini found that:

Seventy-five percent of companies believe that they're customer-centric, while only 30 percent of consumers agree.

Capgemini also reported that 81 percent of customers are willing to pay more for a better experience; in some industries, it goes as high

---

50 "*The Global State of Customer Experience 2019*," CX Network, accessed December 1, 2021, https://www.cxnetwork.com/cx-experience/reports/the-global-state-of-customer-experience-2019

51 "The Disconnected Customer: What Digital Customer Experience Leaders Teach Us about Reconnecting with Customers," Capgemini, June 28, 2017, https://www.capgemini.com/resources/the-disconnected-customer-what-digital-customer-experience-leaders-teach-us-about/

as 87 percent more! We know that there's a linkage between customer experience leaders and stock performance. So focus on the customer, and the numbers (the revenue) will follow.

FOCUS ON THE CUSTOMER

Let's dig into the two reasons behind the customer experience perception gap a bit more.

Acquiring customers can be so much easier than retaining; retention is hard work, and it's a huge part of what a customer experience transformation is all about. But focusing on acquisition can yield a much faster return on investment, especially when companies are driven by growth metrics. (Again, driven by metrics.) Acquisition is easier to track, and there are (almost) immediate returns on your investments.

> It's important to recognize that a customer experience transformation is all about baby steps.

Because retention—and customer experience transformation—work is slow and difficult, people get bored and tend to fall back into their old habits rather than relentlessly driving toward the ultimate goal. It's important to recognize that a customer experience transformation is all about baby steps. In order to keep people energized and focused, share quick wins, and celebrate successes as you progress.

Related to this imbalanced focus on acquisition is the message you send to your employees that starts with *"Revenue is down this quarter. We need all hands on deck focusing on drumming up new business."* Suddenly, all of your customer experience transformation resources are shifted to business development and sales efforts.

Interestingly enough, the first question you should ask is, *Why are sales down?* Is it a quality or performance issue? Is it that you're getting pushed out by your competition? Do you really understand what your customers' needs are?

I've seen this scenario play out a few times, and each time, if the companies would've fixed what was ailing them, then sales numbers wouldn't be down. One particular company had been struggling to grow the business; growth had stalled (even declined), and they asked me to help them get to the root cause. They had some sense of what might be wrong, but oh boy, they honestly had no idea how deep the issues ran. The ten principles I outline in this book? They broke every single one of them.

So we started the work to restore balance in the organization when suddenly everything fell apart. We hadn't even had enough time under our belts to effect real change yet. But the latest quarter's numbers were in, and the CEO wasn't happy. It was time to slash the budget, starting with my contract and the corresponding work that we were doing to right the ship. And all resources were shifted to focus on closing deals. The problem with that is the leaky bucket syndrome I mentioned earlier: if you don't fix what ails your customers when they interact with your brand, focusing on acquisition over retention is all bait and switch. "Let's tell prospects how great we are so that they buy, but once they're in, we'll show them who we really are." It bodes well for no one.

Don't take your eyes off the ball. Stay focused on the customer and the customer experience. Stay focused on the work that you're doing to improve the experience. After all, a poor experience is likely why customers aren't buying.

Metrics can help to rally the troops around the customer—but that's only if they're presented in the right context. It's not the right context if you do the following:

- Mention the score without even talking about the customer and the customer experience. (Yes, this does happen!)
- Game surveys (selecting certain customers, surveying at a specific time when you know scores will be better, offering incentives à la "the car dealer curse," etc.) just to get a score.
- Threaten disciplinary action or lost compensation if an employee doesn't achieve a score, especially if the employee doesn't have a clear line of sight to his impact on the customer experience or understand what the score links to.
- Do tactical things to move the needle rather than think big picture about how to improve the experience.

Here's a timely example of bad behavior when the metric becomes the goal. Again, it's the summer of 2021 as I write this, and one of the hot stories at the moment is how Amazon sellers are hunting down their customers who leave bad reviews[52] and asking them to change or delete their reviews in exchange for refunds or gift cards, sometimes two or three times the value of the original purchase. These sellers are more concerned about keeping their star ratings high than they are about fixing the problem.

How can you avoid the metric becoming the target rather than the indicator? Consider these suggestions:

---

52   "When Amazon Customers Leave Negative Reviews, Some Sellers Hunt Them Down," foxbusiness.com, August 9, 2021, https://www.foxbusiness.com/lifestyle/amazon-customers-negative-reviews-sellers-hunt-them-down

- Talk about customers and what your customers are saying about the company and its products and services.
- Make the metric the last thing you talk about—or don't talk about it at all.
- Tell stories about customer successes and customer pain points.
- Focus on employee behaviors and what it takes to improve the experience.
- Share customer feedback, verbatims, emotions, and what's important to customers.
- Act on the feedback.
- Coach and praise based on feedback and the experience the customer had.
- Focus on customer outcomes first, then on business outcomes.
- Ensure that employees have a clear line of sight to the customer.
- Help employees understand how they contribute to the customer experience.
- Don't compensate for metrics; compensate for behaviors and actions.
- Build a culture where the customer is at the center of all you do and no decisions are made unless you ask, *"What would the customer think of this? How would this help or impact the customer?"* (Since you're reading this book, you've taken a step in the right direction!)

Don't measure for the sake of measuring, and don't listen just for the sake of measuring. Listen because you want to understand the customer and where the experience is falling down (or going well). And then act on what you hear.

The behaviors that drive a focus on the metric are not the behaviors that improve the experience; they only/simply move the needle, giving a false sense of a "superior customer experience." Don't just focus on improving the score; do the work to improve the experience, and the numbers will follow. That is a great segue into the next principle, which is all about customer understanding and why that is the cornerstone of customer-centricity.

DO YOU SEE ...	WHAT TO DO?	OUTCOMES OR BENEFITS
We focus on acquisition over retention.	Shift the focus to have more of a balance between the two.	A better customer experience. Higher retention rates.
We focus on moving the needle; the metric is the target, not the customer.	Shift the focus and the work to improving the experience.	The numbers will come. A better customer experience. Higher retention rates.
We have out-of-touch executives who think we deliver a great customer experience, while our customers disagree.	Get these executives in front of customers. Have them participate or listen in on customer interviews and journey mapping workshops.	A better customer experience. Higher retention and growth rates.

CHAPTER 9

Principle 7—Customer Understanding

By putting forth the effort to better understand the habits, tendencies, and value of each and every one of our customers, you can build better, stronger, and more profitable companies.

—PETER FADER, PROFESSOR OF
MARKETING, THE WHARTON SCHOOL OF
THE UNIVERSITY OF PENNSYLVANIA

When was the last time you—yes, I'm talking to you—spoke to one of your customers?

I could tell you stories about a bunch of brands that don't talk to their customers, but let's focus on one—Victoria's Secret. It's a brand that lost its luster in the last decade or so. The wheels came off, and the brand is splitting from the L Brands mother ship to become its own independent entity. Sales have dwindled in recent years, and CEO Martin Waters acknowledged the following:[53] "We got it wrong. We lost relevance with the modern woman. And she told us very clearly

---

53   Lauren Thomas, "Victoria's Secret Details Comeback Plan after L Brands Split, Admits It Lost Relevance with Women," cnbc.com, July 20, 2021, https://www.cnbc.com/2021/07/20/victorias-secret-details-comeback-plan-after-l-brands-split.html

to change our focus from how people look to how people feel—from being about what he wants to being about what she wants."

They lost touch with their customers. They didn't listen to them or take the time to understand them and their needs and preferences. They were getting feedback that their ads (and their annual Angels runway show) pushed unattainable beauty and body type standards. Customers no longer felt that Victoria's Secret represented their own bodies or their own values of being accepting of all body types.

But here's the problem. As they move through their rebranding, they continue to make the same mistakes. They still aren't listening to customers. And how effective is it for a male CEO to run a woman's lingerie company? Wouldn't the brand be better served led by a woman—someone who understands women? Victoria's Secret continues to think it knows better than its customers, and it's not even led by someone who knows anything about its customers and understands their needs! How can you go "from being about what *he* wants to being about what *she* wants" in this intimates category when your CEO is a man? (The answer, of course, is in this chapter.)

Customers buy for their reasons, not yours.

—ORVEL RAY WILSON

By the way, a little backstory on the brand: it was actually founded in 1977 by a man (Roy Raymond) because he wanted to create a women's lingerie store that made men feel comfortable. That was the beginning of the end!

OK, this chapter isn't about gender issues; it's about customer understanding and why it's so important to delivering a great customer experience—and to business success. Demonstrating that with a story about a brand that's suffering the consequences of not putting the customer at the center of all they do, by not putting the "customer" in *customer* experience, is a good way to kick off this chapter.

Here's the bottom line: **customer understanding is the cornerstone of customer-centricity**! The cornerstone is the first stone set in the construction of a masonry foundation. All other stones will be set in reference to this stone, thus determining the position of the entire structure.

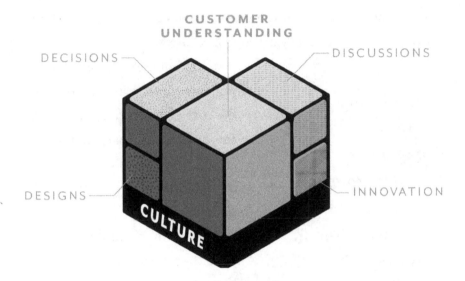

You can't make any improvements, you can't design an experience, and you can't transform anything without customer understanding, without data and insights about your customers. You must first understand customers and their pain points, problems to solve, and jobs to be done.

That understanding must be ingrained in the culture. There must be this foundation (culture) to support and to uphold the fact that understanding is the cornerstone, that it is the catalyst to make changes and to design and deliver the experience your customers desire.

So you can start to see the connection between the foundation—culture—and the cornerstone—customer understanding. Customer understanding feeds the customer-centric culture. It informs it. It must be woven throughout the organization's DNA. And in addition to the values and the behaviors, it drives the culture you want.

WHAT IS CUSTOMER UNDERSTANDING?

Customer understanding is all about learning everything you need to know about your customers (i.e., their needs, their pain points, the jobs they are trying to do, and their current experiences) in order to deliver the experience they expect going forward.

> It's about seeing, feeling, experiencing, and learning through the eyes of the customer, through the customer's heart and mind.

It's about seeing, feeling, experiencing, and learning through the eyes of the customer, through the customer's heart and mind. Sounds like empathy, right? Well, it is—it does build empathy for the customer.

Customer understanding puts the "customer" in *customer* experience, informs your customer experience strategy, and ultimately, drives business growth.

HOW DO YOU ACHIEVE CUSTOMER UNDERSTANDING?

There are really three ways to achieve customer understanding: listen, characterize, and empathize. I mentioned earlier that the first book I wrote is titled *Customer Understanding: Three Ways to Put the "Customer" in Customer Experience (and at the Heart of Your Business)*.

I'll cover each of the three and their importance here, but if you want a more-detailed how-to on this topic, please check out that book.

The graphic below calls out not only the three ways but also illustrates how their data becomes linked through analytics.

While I won't go into as much detail here as in that book, know that the problem with these three approaches—which all work hand in hand—is that if not done correctly (and if you don't do anything with what you learn), you'll be no further ahead in terms of understanding than if you hadn't done them at all.

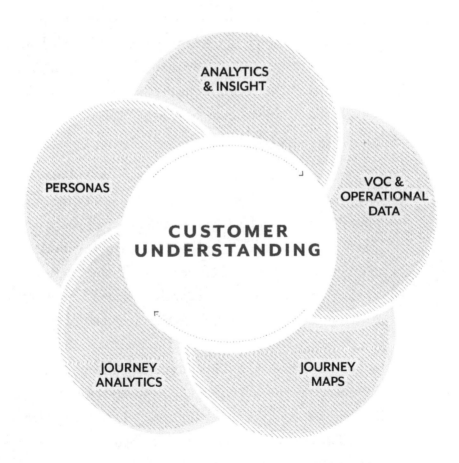

1. **Listen.** The first way to understand customers is to listen. It's really listen, ask, and capture, but ultimately, it's all about listening to customers and hearing what they have said.

   □ **Ask** is about surveys and any other way that you ask for feedback, such as interviews and customer advisory boards.

   □ It's also how you **listen** to customers—wherever they prefer to provide feedback—such as through social media, online reviews, or the feedback they leave with your employees.

   □ And finally, it also includes what I like to refer to as "the bread crumbs of data that customers leave behind as they interact and transact with the brand," which is the data that you **capture** in your systems (point of sale, customer relationship management, contact center, site analytics, etc.) about those interactions and transactions.

   When you marry all of these data sources, it's magical. You can really learn so much about customers, their expectations, attitudes, and behaviors—and how well you're performing against all of that, and then use that to better deliver an experience that meets their needs.

   There are a lot of different channels and ways for customers to tell you about their needs and desired outcomes and how well you are performing against their expectations. Understanding these expectations and identifying key drivers of a great customer experience are important outcomes of this exercise. In a customer-centric organization, every department thirsts for feedback from customers to measure brand awareness, to design products, to improve service offerings, to understand satisfaction levels, and more. Listening is a critical first step to achieving customer understanding.

> *You learn when you listen. You earn when you listen—not just money, but respect.*

—HARVEY MACKAY

2. **Characterize.** The second way to understand customers is to characterize. This is all about developing personas, which are artifacts that describe and represent a behavioral grouping of customers and are specific to your business, not to the industry. The descriptions include vivid narratives, images, and other details that help companies understand who their customers are, understand the needs of the customer and her pain points and problems to solve, and outline motivations, goals, behaviors, challenges, likes, dislikes, objections, and interests that drive buying (or other) decisions.

    How does your company define or segment customers? Do you talk about "profiles" or "target segments" or "target customers" or "target demographics?" Guess what? Your customers are not "target" anything. If you want to design an experience for your customers, whom you've deemed to be men between the ages of eighteen and forty-nine, for example, you're dead wrong. Your customers will be sadly disappointed, and your products and your business will suffer.

    What you need are personas—not just profiles or segments. Personas are fictional characters that are created to represent customer types based on similar needs, pain points, problems to be solved, jobs to be done, preferences, expectations, goals, and more. Personas are research based, created by starting with customer interviews and then fine-tuned with validation surveys. Do not allow personas to be developed in your organization with internal thinking (because you think you know who your customers are). It perpetuates inside-out thinking. It's not accurate. And it's lazy. You have to talk to customers. After all, it's called customer understanding, not business understanding or thinking.

When it comes to designing the customer experience, personas take us closer to the individual customer's desires than anything can, short of customizing or personalizing for the individual. Experiences are designed at a macro level for each persona, making the job easier then for frontline folks to tweak and fine-tune the experience at the individual level as they interact with the customer.

3. **Empathize.** The third way to achieve customer understanding is what I refer to as empathizing. It is all about walking in your customers' shoes—with your customers—and getting inside their heads and hearts to really understand the experience they are having with your brand today. I'm talking about journey mapping. When you create journey maps, customers are telling you what they are doing, thinking, and feeling as they complete some interaction or transaction with your brand.

Journey mapping is a learning exercise. Companies learn about their customers and about the experience they put them through to interact with the business. And that learning allows them to become more customer-centric and more aware of the experiences they create for their customers. That's just the beginning. While journey maps themselves are tools, I've developed a six-step process to ensure that the maps become the catalysts for change that they are meant to be. The process goes like this:

1. *Plan:* Fail to plan, plan to fail. This step includes all the prep work to get ready for the journey mapping workshop, including identifying the personas for which you'll map; the objectives, scope, outcomes, and success metrics of the map; and the workshop participants (stakeholders and customers). This step may also include data gathering and customer interviews.

2. *Empathize:* In this step, you'll map what customers are doing, thinking, and feeling; add data and metrics into the map to help identify moments of truth; bring the map to life with artifacts (e.g., pictures, videos, and documents); and assign owners to the customer's steps.

3. *Identify:* Next up, it's important to prioritize moments of truth, research issues, conduct root cause analysis, develop action plans, and assign owners and deadlines to the plans.

4. *Introspect:* An important step that many skip is to look inward and create a service blueprint and a process map to correspond with the customer journey you've mapped. You can't fix what's happening on the outside, what the customer is experiencing, if you don't fix what's happening behind the scenes.

5. *Ideate:* In this step, you conduct future state mapping workshops, ideate solutions for customer and backstage pain points, and design the future state experience.

6. *Implement:* In this final step, you'll prototype and test the new experience design—and fail fast; implement the

new experience; share the maps and train employees; close the loop with customers; and update maps to reflect the new current experience.

LINKING THE THREE WAYS

All three of these approaches to achieve customer understanding are closely linked. Both listening (feedback) and characterizing (personas) result in a lot of data that feed into the maps (empathizing). Here's some proof.

MyCustomer.com conducted research in 2018[54] in which they uncovered two interesting stats:

- Sixty percent of companies that don't journey map are not satisfied with the insights they have into customer journeys.

  □ They are only surveying or using other listening posts.

- Eighty-nine percent of companies that use journey maps are satisfied or very satisfied with the insights.

  □ They conduct customer research, incorporate voice-of-the-customer feedback, and enrich their maps with customer data.

These three customer understanding concepts are critical learning exercises. You walk away from each one of them with a lot of knowledge about customers and about the experience they desire. When combined, you are so much wiser and have a greater under-

---

54   "Customer Journey Mapping Research Report 2018: A Global Study Examining Maturity and Best Practices," mycustomer.com, accessed December 1, 2021, https://www.mycustomer.com/resources/customer-journey-mapping-research-report-2018

standing of customers and of the work that lies ahead to deliver on their needs and expectations. And that is key: you've got to do something with what you learn. This action is where customer understanding manifests itself into customer-centricity and becomes the cornerstone for it.

> *Don't measure anything unless the data helps you make a better decision or change your actions. If you're not prepared to change your diet or your workouts, don't get on the scale.*

> —SETH GODIN

At no time in history have you ever had access to so much data and had so many opportunities to do what's right by and for the customer as a result of having that data. The problem for brands today—beyond *not* embarking on the journey to understand customers—seems to also lie in disparate systems, data accessibility, and data quality. The customer experience advantage goes to the companies that can bring it all together to ultimately deliver the right data to the right people at the right time to deliver the right experience for the customers in front of them.

DATA IS JUST DATA …

Taking action on what you learn as you do this customer understanding work is a critical next step. Data is just data until you do something with it.

As I mentioned earlier in the chapter, the problems when it comes to all of this understanding work are not only in

> **Taking action on what you learn as you do this customer understanding work is a critical next step.**

doing the work incorrectly but also in *not* doing anything with what you've learned. In the end, businesses are challenged not only with the aforementioned disparate systems, data accessibility, and data quality but also with how to transform the data into useful insights.

I have six steps to follow to transform the data into a usable format and then consume it.

1. Data must be *centralized*. Data are useless to improving the customer experience when they remain siloed; siloed data mean siloed experiences. You cannot deliver a personalized customer experience across your various channels if the data are housed in several disparate systems. You need a way to bring the data together in one place so that they can be analyzed in a sane way.

2. Data must be *analyzed*. Analysis takes many forms because there will be many different types of data to make sense of. You'll need a way to cross-tab, predict, identify key drivers, and prioritize improvements with survey data; mine and analyze your unstructured data; and track, review, and prioritize social media inputs and influencers. You'll conduct linkage analysis to link customer and employee data, customer feedback with operational metrics, and all data to financial measures. And you'll need to conduct a root cause analysis to understand the why behind it all.

3. Data must be *synthesized*. Once data have been broken down and analyzed for better understanding, they are most useful for the end user when transformed into insights. Put all the pieces of the analysis together to tell a story, to put it into context for those who need to act on it—a story that can be easily understood and translated into a better customer experience.

4. Data must be *socialized*. Those insights and their corresponding stories must be shared across the organization and in such a way that people know what to do with them. Insights and resultant recommendations must get into the hands of the right people who will do something with them.

5. Data must be *strategized*. To strategize means to define your strategy or your action plan, and in this case, it involves both tactical (how you'll respond to each and every customer) and strategic (how the business will respond, including operational, product, and process changes) measures. This is where we begin to turn insights into action.

6. Data must be *operationalized*. Ensure that you have the right feedback at the right time from the right customers, then glean insights, create action plans, and drive them all back to the right departments and right employees who take action at the right touch points at the right time. Then close the loop on your own change management process: track and measure your efforts in order to maintain a continuous improvement cycle.

The following graphic outlines how you combine the customer understanding work with these six steps to go from data to insights to advantage.

FIVE STEPS FROM DATA TO ADVANTAGE

 DATA

Define Objectives
Listen
Characterize
Empathize
Gather
Centralize

 INSIGHT

Analyze
Synthesize
Contextualize

 ACTION

Socialize
Uncover Root Causes
Develop Action Plan
Operationalize
Close the Loop

 OUTCOMES

For the
business
and the
customer

 **ADVANTAGE**

Outperform:
Expectations
Competitors
Market

In the end, that's what it's all about. Customer understanding allows you to develop products for your customers, to design experiences that meet customer needs and help them do some job, to create value for customers and for the business, and to achieve that ultimate, winning advantage.

The math is simple. Understand customers. Stand out. Outperform your competitors and the market. Delight employees, customers, and ultimately, shareholders.

I started the chapter with a story about a brand that doesn't listen to customers. Let's close this one out with a brand that does listen. Atom Bank is an online-only bank based in the United Kingdom, and their purpose is to be the most customer-centric bank on the planet. Here's just one example of how they listen to their customers, use what they learn to improve the experience, and reap the benefits as a business.

Atom customers were having problems accepting their mortgage offers within the bank's app. The app was confusing, and it was difficult to find where to accept the offer. Atom listened to customer feedback and transformed the app to simplify the process. As a result, they reduced the call volume into their contact center, which was expensive because of the number of calls, the length of the calls, and the potential lost customers among those who didn't call.

According to Michael Sherwood, head of customer experience at Atom Bank,[55] "If you understand the reasons customers are calling and fix the things that are driving the contact in the first place, then you reduce the cost associated with answering the query. If you keep

---

55   Leigh Peacock-Goodwin, "We're Obsessed with Customer Experience! An Interview with
      Michael Sherwood," Atom Bank, May 17, 2019, https://www.atombank.co.uk/blog/2019/
      were-obsessed-with-customer-experience-an-interview-with-michael-sherwood/

improving on the things that matter most to customers, realizing the business benefit becomes a self-fulfilling prophecy."

In August 2021, they reported their first profitable quarter. (While they were founded in 2013, Atom didn't officially launch as a bank until November 2015.) It pays to listen to—and to understand—your customers!

Taking action on the learnings of your customer understanding work is not optional. In the next chapter, I'll go into some detail about how we ensure everyone is involved in taking action.

DO YOU SEE ...	WHAT TO DO?	OUTCOMES OR BENEFITS
We haven't developed personas and focus on target demographics.	Do the work. Develop customer personas.	Understanding. Empathy. A greater ability to design the experience for customers.
We are listening to customers but aren't doing anything with the learnings.	Stop focusing on the metric. Start focusing on improving the experience based on customer feedback.	Better customer experience. Growth. Advocacy. Loyalty.
We haven't mapped the customer journey with customers.	Walk in customers' shoes. Identify where the experience is broken. Fix it.	Better customer experience. Empathy. Growth. Advocacy. Loyalty.

CHAPTER 10

Principle 8—Governance Bridges Organizational Gaps

Good governance cannot remain merely a philosophy.
Concrete steps have to be taken for realizing its goals.

—NARENDRA MODI

I have a confession. This chapter was not originally in the final manuscript I submitted to the publisher. It was a major brain fart. Seriously, every time I talk about customer-centricity and building a customer-centric culture, this topic is always a part of the conversation. How could I forget it?

Especially since, if I had a dollar for every time someone asked me how to bridge the gaps between various departments in an organization or how to break down or connect silos or how to get that grassroots groundswell among employees to really transform an organization, I'd be rich.

So I woke up one morning just sweating it. "Oh, boy. I really messed this up. This is an important part of the work that needs to be done to build a winning organization. How could I have forgotten about this?" Luckily, thankfully, I'm here to tell you that the concept made it into the book.

155

What is this important foundational element? **Governance.**

I know. Most people think scary things when they hear that word, but in this case, it's the "good governance." People immediately assume that "governance" is only referring to a governing body, including people, roles, and responsibilities, that informs and lends oversight to the work that lies ahead. The grumblings sound something like "Great. More oversight. Can't I just be left alone to do my job?"

> Governance bridges the gap between departments. It helps to break down and connect silos.

BusinessDictionary.com used to define governance as

The establishment of policies, and continuous monitoring of their proper implementation, by the members of the governing body of an organization. It includes the mechanisms required to balance the powers of the members (with the associated accountability), and their primary duty of enhancing the prosperity and viability of the organization.

That doesn't sound so scary, does it?

It's important to customer-centricity because customer-centricity is and must be organization-wide. It's cross-functional. It has no walls or boundaries. As I mentioned previously, by definition, customer-centric cultures are collaborative cultures, and there can be no collaboration if silos exist—or if silos are not connected. How can employees work together with their colleagues if these silos prevent them from doing so?

There are really two parts to this "good governance:" in short, oversight and execution. And neither is scary.

1. **The structure:** It's all about the governing body but also about establishing policies, monitoring the organization, and

enhancing its prosperity. This part covers both oversight and execution, as well as driving accountability throughout the organization by creating committees and assigning specific tasks and responsibilities to those committees.

2. **The operating model:** It's also an operating model that drives the execution of the customer experience vision to strategy through data democratization, socializing and operationalizing insights to action, prioritizing improvement initiatives, developing new business processes, defining success metrics, outlining the decision-making process, defining the communication plan, and more.

The two parts work together to ensure that the organization works together toward a common cause, goal, and/or outcome. Governance bridges the gap between departments. It helps to break down and connect silos. It's also the best source of that grassroots groundswell to get everyone involved.

> *Breaking an old business model is always going to require leaders to follow their instinct. There will always be persuasive reasons not to take a risk. But if you only do what worked in the past, you will wake up one day and find that you've been passed by.*

—CLAYTON CHRISTENSEN

GOVERNANCE PART 1: THE STRUCTURE

Let's start with the structure, which stands in the form of committees that must be cross-functional in order to avoid siloed efforts and thinking overtaking work that needs to be done. The role of the committees, in a nutshell, is to keep the entire organization focused on improving the customer experience and doing what's right for customers.

At a high level, the committees have a variety of responsibilities that make them critical to success, not the least of which includes commitment and alignment from the top (see the "Executive Committee" section), which happens to be what you read about in chapter 4 about principle 2. Committees do the following:

- Provide oversight into the various customer experience improvement initiatives, and provide guidance and prioritization with regard to each.
- Define criteria for prioritization, metrics to track progress, and overall success metrics.
- Monitor the progress of the initiatives toward meeting business objectives and desired outcomes.
- Review customer insights, and ensure that they are not only disseminated to the respective departments but also operationalized.
- Provide oversight to ensure cross-functional teams work together and share responsibility for improvements.
- Maintain a master list of customer experience initiatives not only for the purpose of monitoring but also to use when prioritizing new initiatives against the current workload.
- Review, prioritize, and approve the budget for customer experience improvement initiatives.
- Drive grassroots adoption of the work to be done, and facilitate that groundswell needed to ensure success organization-wide.

There are various committees that can be included in a governance structure, and roles and responsibilities will vary somewhat by committee. The most common committees and roles in the structure include an executive committee, a CX executive sponsor, an EX (employee experience) executive sponsor, a core CX team, CX champions, and a culture committee.

Is there a reporting structure to these committees? This graphic is the best way to visualize that.

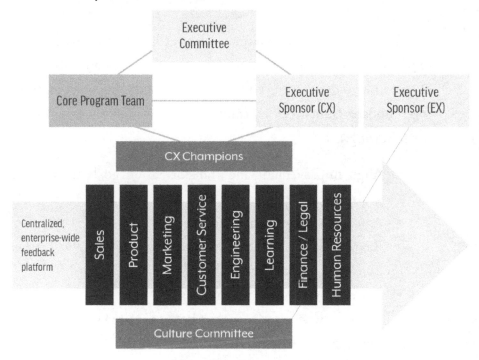

At the top, above the executive committee, would be the CEO. The individual committees regularly provide updates to the other committees, and where the work of one overlaps closely with another, I have them nominate a representative to attend the opening of the other committee's meeting for a quick update/information sharing.

Let's look at each one of those in more detail.

EXECUTIVE COMMITTEE

The executive committee is comprised of key executives in your organization; this can include department heads, business unit heads, and other business leaders (C or V level) deemed essential to successful outcomes. I would recommend that your CFO be a part of this committee; it may not be necessary for him or her to sit in on every meeting, but having insight into the various initiatives early on will certainly help when it comes time to prioritize and to get budget approval.

This committee will maintain a master list of organization-wide projects and initiatives, including those specific to initiatives born out of customer understanding efforts. The committee will meet monthly to get updates from the other committees, at which time they will do the following:

- Align improvement and transformation goals to business goals.
- Agree on success criteria and metrics.
- Review, prioritize, and approve initiatives to be further developed and designed.
- Review and approve action plans.
- Identify owners, additional resources required to execute, and the budget for these initiatives.
- Provide budget, resources, and guardrails for execution, as needed.
- Empower the committees and respective teams/resources to implement the initiatives.
- Drive accountability for delivery of insights and action plans across functions.

The executive committee has ultimate oversight into all things customer experience, obviously. They hold the keys to transformation success.

EXECUTIVE SPONSORS

I mentioned earlier that there are two types of executive sponsors, CX and EX. Ideally, this role would be handled by one individual, but it seems more fitting to have a separate sponsor to champion customer experience work and one for employee experience work. Rarely have I found that both customer experience and employee experience oversight and responsibilities fall with one individual. Usually, that falls with the CCO or vice president of CX for customer experience and with the chief human resources officer or vice president of HR, people and culture, etc. for employee experience. These two individuals must partner and work together. I've already written about how employee experience drives customer experience.

Regardless of where the function resides, their roles are the same. They are the first lines of defense for their respective areas of oversight, and they are champions for their constituents (i.e., customers and employees, respectively) across the organization. They are responsible for developing the vision, strategy, and road map for their work and have oversight of their staff and teams to drive execution of the work to be done. They are "uniters" within the organization, educating and bringing everyone together for—and aligning them with—a common cause and purpose. They must ensure that the customer and the impact on the customer is embedded in all discussions, decisions, and designs throughout the organization.

CORE CX TEAM

The core CX team is comprised of the staff that does the critical underlying CX work and keeps the CX engine humming, so to speak. At a high level, this team does the following, and more:

- Develop, implement, and manage tools and processes to understand customers.

- Cocreate and design new experiences with customers.
- Centralize, analyze, and synthesize customer feedback and data.
- Identify metrics to track, and ensure those metrics are linked to business outcomes.
- Share the insights from the customer understanding tools throughout the organization.
- Develop the strategy to achieve the desired and intended customer experience.
- Prepare internal and external communications about the work that is being done

The work that they do feeds, informs, and supports the last two committees.

CX CHAMPIONS

This is a cross-functional committee, with representation from each department. Having that cross-functional representation helps break down or connect silos and allows for each department's voice, feedback, and perspectives to be brought to—and heard by—the committee. Committee members focus on CX improvements and changes that must originate or occur in their respective business areas. They educate their colleagues and are the conduits from their departments to the committee at large, and vice versa.

Within committee meetings, they represent their departments and are subject matter experts on customer needs and business processes stemming from their individual departments. In this regard, they also become an extension of the core CX team, as the core staff cannot and does not have the insights into each department's area of expertise and how that contributes to the experience overall.

Committee members drive the work within their departments, first by educating and then by socializing feedback and insights received. Ultimately, they facilitate and champion change initiatives within their departments. The individual departments are then responsible for completing a root cause analysis, identifying improvements to be made, and providing all the details to get those improvements prioritized and approved by the executive committee. Remember that the core CX team can only ensure that the insights are delivered to the various departments that need to act on them. The actual customer experience improvements are completed by the responsible departments.

CULTURE COMMITTEE

A culture committee is also a group of cross-functional employees who meet to identify, discuss, and plan ways to promote and to drive the desired culture throughout the organization. You absolutely have to have cross-functional representation on this committee as well, as that diversity ensures that no one area of the company has greater influence over culture development and change than any other.

This group of like-minded (as in, aligned with the culture you desire) individuals live and breathe the company's core values and culture. They have a ground-level view of "how things work" in the company, and they identify, discuss, and plan ways to promote and drive the desired culture.

The committee helps to create that groundswell of adoption of the culture traits as defined by the core values and corresponding behaviors, as mentioned in principle 1. One of the most important things that they do is socialize, operationalize, and model the core values. They also brainstorm and develop programs and events (e.g., fun, educational, or health/wellness events) that bring employees together to build and support the culture. The committee may even help to define (or revisit) the core values, and if you haven't yet defined acceptable behaviors aligned with each value, they can undertake that exercise too.

Committee members are also a conduit between their departments and this committee, as well as the executive committee. They must talk to fellow employees to keep a pulse on the culture and what's happening in the workplace. With this information, they can identify ways to support the evolution of the culture or mitigate its erosion.

A bad system will beat a good person every time.

—W. EDWARDS DEMING

GOVERNANCE PART 2: THE OPERATING MODEL

All right, on to the second part, the operating model. That operating model is your bridge between the strategy and its execution. Wikipedia defines an operating model as *"an abstract and visual representation (model) of how an organization delivers value to its customers or beneficiaries as well as how an organization actually runs itself."*[56] It's how you will operate, how you will execute, and how you will fulfill your vision. Ultimately, it's how you will operationalize your strategy.

There's a customer experience vision (closely linked to the corporate vision—or it is also the corporate vision) that must be in place as the predecessor to a customer experience strategy. The strategy outlines how you'll execute against that vision. But the strategy itself must have some foundational elements in place in order for you to execute it. Within the governance operating model, you'll outline how things will get done to achieve your desired outcomes.

---

56   "Operating model," Wikipedia, accessed December 1, 2021, https://en.wikipedia.org/wiki/Operating_model

The operating model portion of governance includes various components, including people, processes, a measurement framework, and tools and technology.

PEOPLE

Yes, people are included as part of the operating model, even though we define and outline committees, people, roles, and responsibilities in the structure. While the people outlined for the structure provide oversight and are conduits to the rest of the organization, we need to identify the individuals or the teams within each cross-functional area who will take ownership of the actual improvement work and projects to be completed. In this operating model, we've got to outline how they will be supported, what the general approach will be, and how we'll measure success. We've also got to specify roles, responsibilities, and decision rights.

Change is not an event; it's a process.

—CHERYL JAMES

MEASUREMENT FRAMEWORK

The measurement framework includes, as you would imagine, all the ways that you measure the customer experience, the employee experience, market(ing) research, outcomes, and success. This includes your voice-of-the-customer program and how that feedback will be used, persona research and how the personas will be used, journey mapping workshops and how the findings will be used, and other data sources, including what I call "the bread crumbs of data that customers leave behind as they interact and transact with your brand." (You just read about all of these in the previous chapter on principle 7, customer understanding.)

Within the governance operating model, you'll outline how things will get done to achieve your desired outcomes.

Not only is the framework about the data and the various sources, but it's also about where the data is housed, how it will be analyzed, who needs it, how it will be used, and specific data and insight democratization rules.

And finally, the framework will also outline key performance indicators and success metrics—all clearly linked to desired outcomes for the customer, the employee, and the business—and how they were selected.

PROCESSES

Clearly defined processes and procedures are key to the success of any strategy. How will the outcome be achieved? There are a host of different processes and workflows that must be outlined as part of your governance operating model, not the least of which include the following.

- *Decision-making process:* How will decisions (approvals, priorities, resource, budget, project plans, etc.) be made about the work to be done?
- *Prioritization process:* How will you prioritize the work to be done? What algorithm will you use to prioritize? What are the factors in that algorithm?
- *Workflow process:* How will people work together to achieve a common goal? Or to deliver on the desired outcome?
- *Communication plan:* How will you communicate to employees and to customers about what you're doing, what it means for them, and what the desired outcomes are?
- *Training process:* How will you train both employees and customers on the new experience?
- *Policies:* What policies must be in place to guide the decisions made and actions taken in order to drive toward the desired outcome?
- *Adoption and alignment processes:* How will we get the entire organization on board with what we are trying to accomplish?
- *Other specific processes:* In the measurement framework, I mentioned that you're going to outline how the data will be used, who has access, etc. Any other processes that must be clearly outlined in order to execute the strategy must also be defined as part of the operating model.

Note that when these (and other) processes and workflows are clearly outlined, there should be no question about who does what and why. And there should be either a clear connection or a breakdown of silos to ensure the work is executed properly.

In addition, it's interesting to note that your core values should kick in here. No processes, procedures, or policies should be designed or implemented without ensuring that they are in alignment with—and reinforce—your core values.

TOOLS AND TECHNOLOGY

One final and important component of the governance operating model is tools and technology. What will your CX tech stack look like? What tools do you need in order to gather and to analyze the data? What technology will you need to disseminate the data and insights? What technology will the company at large require in order to use the data and insights that have been shared? How will you determine which technology to use and who gets access/needs to use it?

As you can see, there is a complex set of decisions and processes that are critical to the success of your transformation strategy. If you truly want to bring the organization together, if you truly want to bridge the gaps between key departments, you've got to establish governance. Showing employees that they can and should work together and giving them the chance and the ownership to do so does bring the organization together to work toward a common goal.

We should work on our processes, not the outcome of our processes.

—W. EDWARDS DEMING

I know. This was a heavy chapter with a lot of detail compared to other chapters. For the next principle, we'll delve deep into the DNA of the organization and focus on how you think and act differently on the inside when you're a customer-centric organization.

DO YOU SEE …	WHAT TO DO?	OUTCOMES OR BENEFITS
Departments working in silos when they should be collaborating with others?	Reiterate that there are no physical walls between departments. Model it. Encourage participation in governance committees.	Increased employee productivity and satisfaction. Consistent customer experience.
Silos that can't/ won't break down or connect?	Create cross-functional teams to solve for X. Create opportunities to collaborate and share the results of collaboration efforts.	Increased employee productivity and satisfaction. Consistent customer experience.
Only pockets of employees who embrace the core values and the customer-centric culture?	Have culture committee members work with these employees. What's keeping them from embracing the values?	Strong culture. Culture erosion mitigation. Better employee experience.

CHAPTER 11

Principle 9—Outside In versus Inside Out

The most customer-centric organizations can answer any question by deciding what's best for the customer, without ever having to ask.

—AARON LEVIE

I was sitting in a client's conference room with a group of leaders one day. The conversation was lively as we talked about the customer experience work we (they) were about to embark upon. The conversation evolved to how we were going to understand their customers. We had just finished going through the details about the approaches we would take to listen, characterize, and empathize when I kept hearing, "We think our customers are …" or "I think our customers want …" or simply, "We think customers …" I paused the conversation and said, "Every time you start a sentence with 'We/I think customers …' I need you to put a dollar in the jar at the center of the table."

Seriously. There is no "we *think*." It has to be "we *know*" because you've done the work to know, to understand. This is really what being customer-centric is all about. No guesses. You know because you know. Because you did the work and you brought what you learned into every discussion, decision, and design. If you didn't do the work, you're thinking and behaving in a very inside-out manner.

What do I mean by that?

Inside-out thinking and doing means your focus is on processes, systems, tools, and products that are designed and implemented based on internal thinking and intuition. The customer's needs, jobs to be done, and perspectives do not play a part in this type of thinking and doing; they aren't taken into consideration. You make decisions because you *think* it's what's best for the business—not for customers. Or you think you know what's best for customers.

On the other hand, **outside-in thinking and doing** means that you look at your business from the customer's perspective and subsequently design processes, tools, and products and make decisions based on what's best for the customer, what solves problems for the customer, and what creates value for the customer. You make decisions because you know it's what's best for your customers. Why? Because you listen to them and you understand them and the jobs they are trying to do.

Here's a simple example of inside-out thinking and doing.

My internet provider was working on upgrading their service earlier this week, and it resulted in an outage (apparently) from midnight until 6:00 a.m. I'm usually up around 5:30 a.m., so when I discovered I couldn't connect, I thought that it might just be my router. I went through the standard unplug-everything-to-reset-the-service rigmarole to no avail. So I called customer service to see if there was a larger system outage and if not, to get some assistance. I was immediately authenticated by their interactive voice response system because of the phone number I was calling from. I then had to go through several prompts to get to technical support, only to hear a message that there would be an outage from midnight to 6:00 a.m. as a result of the work they were doing.

Whew. I'm exhausted just typing that story. Simple solution. Simple shift to outside-in thinking and doing. Think about your customers and how your decisions impact them. What would your customers tell you right now? They would say, "Communicate proactively with me. Set my expectations." Instead, I spent (wasted) twenty minutes only to hear that message at the end. Wouldn't it have been easier if they had texted or emailed customers in advance to let them know that there would be an outage? But what they did was what *they thought* was best—for them, certainly not for me or any other customer.

If you're guilty of doing these types of things in your business, then you're definitely not using outside-in thinking and doing.

WHAT'S THE DIFFERENCE?

You'll know when you're operating inside-out versus outside-in. Here's what each looks like in the business.

It might be **inside-out thinking and doing** when there's a conscious decision to make process, policy, people, systems, or other changes that:

1. don't improve the customer experience at the same time;
2. are about maximizing shareholder returns, not about benefits for the customer;
3. improve internal efficiencies but to the detriment of customer interactions;
4. are cost-cutting measures that also negatively impact the customer experience; and

5. might be the wrong process, policy, people, or systems to change.

By contrast, **outside-in thinking and doing** flips each of those points on its head and looks like this. There's a conscious decision to make process, policy, people, systems, or other changes that:

1. improve the customer experience at the same time;
2. are about maximizing benefits for the customer, which will result in benefits for the shareholder;
3. improve internal efficiencies known to be pain points when executing customer interactions;
4. are cost-cutting measures that significantly improve the customer experience; and
5. are the right process, policy, people, or systems because you've listened to customer feedback and know how customers are affected.

It's clear that **outside-in thinking and doing** is the way to go. It leads to a number of things, none of which you'll get by making decisions that are not based on what's best for your customers:

- reduced complaints,
- increased satisfaction,
- increased referrals,
- increased repeat purchases,
- improved ease of doing business, and
- fewer lost customers.

These then translate to reduced costs and increased revenue for the business.

WEAVING THE CUSTOMER INTO YOUR COMPANY'S DNA

How can you ensure that you're operating in an **outside-in** manner? Here are some tips.

- Understand customers and what they are trying to do, and use that understanding to develop products for the customer, products that solve their problems and help them do what they are trying to do.
- Listen to customers at all key touch points, close the loop with customers on their feedback, and act on what you hear.
- Share the feedback, and ensure it's used throughout the organization to make decisions and to design the best experience for your customers.
- Do right by the customer; ask "Is this decision what's best for the customer?"
- Reduce customer effort rather than making the experience convoluted and confusing.
- Save a seat in the room (à la Jeff Bezos's empty chair) for the customer/customer's voice.
- Map customer journeys, and ensure all employees—frontline and back office—have a clear line of sight to how they impact the customer experience.
- Talk about customers and what they are saying.

The customer and her voice need to be incorporated into all decisions, designs, and development. Weave the customer throughout your organization's DNA, and watch what happens.

Change the language, change the conversation, and change the culture.

How do you do that? How do you ensure that the customer is always front and center in your conversations and decision-making process?

Jeff Bezos popularized the concept of having an empty chair in his executive meetings. That empty chair represents the customer to ensure that the customer and her voice are included in every decision. I've got clients who have taken the concept and evolved it a bit, painting the chairs, using teddy bears to represent customers, and just decorating the chairs to make sure no one overlooks them. Howard Schultz expanded on the concept, too, and had two empty chairs in his staff meetings: one to represent the employee and one to represent the customer.

I've visited Airbnb headquarters a couple of times. They keep customers—both hosts and guests—top of mind in a few different ways. First, their conference rooms and meeting areas are fashioned after actual guest locations. Each area has a placard that explains who the host is, where the host is located, and why they became a host. Then they've got pictures of hosts and guests around their offices, again, telling the stories of who they are and why they host or why they stay at an Airbnb facility.

How can you bring the customer into the business every day? Here are some ideas:

- Have an empty chair in meetings to represent the customer.
- Share customer data/insights.
- Talk about customers before metrics.
- Hang personas on every wall.
- Create persona animations to introduce and socialize them.
- Tell stories about each persona.
- Hang customer pictures on your walls.
- Place customer cutouts in the office.
- Bring real customers into your meetings/offices.

- Stream customer feedback on monitors.
- Share customer interviews and videos.
- Hang journey maps on your walls.
- Create a journey walk/gallery.
- Build out a customer room.
- Hire a CCO and team of CX professionals.

Here's a really interesting example from LEGO. They actually hired some of their customers. If you know LEGO, you know that they are hyperfocused on their customers and innovate with them on a regular basis. But one thing they discovered about their own brick designers was that they were great at design but weren't very good at LEGO. They designed cool products that customers weren't interested in. To solve that problem, they figured that some of their customers must also be great designers. This was true. There were some great designers among their customer base; they were hired and designed winning products. Now when they hire designers, they must already be active LEGO users/builders too.

Customer-centric companies have to find ways to weave the customer voice into their daily operations across departments, business lines, divisions, etc.—across the entire organization. Then and only then will they be in a position to innovate, to drive continuous improvement, and to create value for customers and for the business.

People don't want to buy a quarter-inch drill.
They want a quarter-inch hole!

—THEODORE LEVITT

Those naysayers who pooh-pooh this whole concept of outside-in are the ones who think customers don't know what they want.

They believe *they* know best what customers want and need. Two classic examples are Steve Jobs, who had a reputation for not wanting to do customer research (although Apple was a client of mine years ago, and they actually do listen to customers), and Henry Ford, who said that if he'd asked customers what they wanted, they'd have said, "Faster horses."

If you're asking them what they want, you're doing it all wrong. Focus on their pain points, problems to solve, and jobs to be done; that's what you need to ask about. That's the voice that you need to bring into the organization to ensure you build products for customers rather than finding customers for your products. When you think of it in that way, you realize that "faster horses" is really the customer's way of telling you that the current mode of transportation is an issue, that it's slow and not meeting their needs. What they need is a mode that gets them to their destination much faster. Enter the Model T. (Although twenty years earlier, Ford had built the quadricycle.)

> **Focus on their pain points, problems to solve, and jobs to be done; that's what you need to ask about.**

This quote from Harvard Business School Professor Theodore Levitt rings true here: "People don't want to buy a quarter-inch drill. They want a quarter-inch hole!" The problem being solved by the product is the customer's need for a quarter-inch hole. When you take the time to bring the customer's voice into all you do, you solve problems for your customers and create value for them. And that sells a lot more products than creating something no one wants.

In the next chapter, I'll take you through the final foundational principle, which is closely tied to this concept of outside-in thinking and doing.

DO YOU SEE ...	WHAT TO DO?	OUTCOMES OR BENEFITS
Decisions are being made based on what leaders think customers need or based on what's best for the business.	Do the customer understanding work. Bring the customer and her voice into all discussions, decisions, and designs.	Better customer experience. Advocacy. Loyalty. Growth.
Policies and processes are designed without consideration for the impact on the customer.	Bring the customer voice into designing policies and procedures. Be sure to ask how they will impact the customer.	Better customer experience for employees and customers. Advocacy. Loyalty. Growth.
We are asking customers what they want.	Flip the script, and ask customers about their pain points, problems to solve, and jobs to be done.	Better customer experience. Advocacy. Loyalty. Growth.

CHAPTER 12

Principle 10—Forget the Golden Rule

Your website isn't the center of your universe. Your Facebook page isn't the center of your universe. Your mobile app isn't the center of your universe. The customer is the center of your universe.

—BRUCE ERNST

In *How to Win Friends & Influence People*, Dale Carnegie shares this story in a chapter that talks about how to arouse in others an eager *want*: "I often went fishing up in Maine during the summer. Personally I am very fond of strawberries and cream, but I have found that for some strange reason, fish prefer worms. So when I went fishing, I didn't think about what I wanted. I thought about what they wanted. I didn't bait the hook with strawberries and cream. Rather, I dangled a worm or grasshopper in front of the fish and said: 'Wouldn't you like to have that?'" To that he adds: "Why not use the same common sense when fishing for people?"

Basically, why push onto others what *we* want? Instead, take the time to listen and to understand the person in front of you—and give them what *they* want. Rather than assuming that everyone is like you, realize that different people have different tastes, wants, desires, needs, etc. This last principle feels like a good culmination of the last several principles—it puts the exclamation point on the entire concept of customer-centricity: **forget the Golden Rule and live (and do business) by the Platinum Rule.**

It's an age-old debate … gold or platinum?

I know. I know. The Golden Rule dates back to the Bible. And over the years in this profession, I've heard so many people not only refer to the Golden Rule but also revere it. But it's got to change. It doesn't make sense. The way one person or one group wants to be treated isn't necessarily the same way the other person or group wants to be treated. So let's treat others the way *they* want to be treated.

While the Golden Rule ignores the feelings of others and assumes that we all want to be treated the same way, the Platinum Rule recognizes that we don't, that everyone wants to be treated the way *they* want to be treated. It's quite the improvement to the Golden Rule. It's much more empathetic.

Put differently, I think the Golden Rule perpetuates inside-out thinking and doing, while the Platinum Rule inspires outside-in thinking and doing. Honestly, this last principle really is a combination of most of the other principles. If we put others first, they have a great experience, and the business wins!

> *The quickest way to profits is to serve the customer*
> *in the way the customer wants to be served.*
>
> —ALFRED P. SLOAN, FORMER CHAIRMAN
> OF GENERAL MOTORS

One of the books that I regularly recommend to leaders is Hal Rosenbluth's *The Customer Comes Second.*[57] The book was written in 1992, but it still applies in so many ways today, even when he writes about technology and the challenges of technology back then. It's amazing to read that and realize that things aren't really much different today! That seems crazy to say thirty years later, especially when we think about the evolution of technology. But I digress. This story isn't about technology; it's about being human and putting yourself in your customer's shoes.

One particular story he shares in the book is so relevant to this Platinum Rule principle. He and his wife frequent a certain restaurant for breakfast. Waitstaff typically set the tables and serve food and drinks for right-handed patrons. Hal, however, is left handed, and he's used to rearranging the silverware and cups or glasses to accommodate the fact that he's a southpaw.

> **If we put others first, they have a great experience, and the business wins!**

But at this particular restaurant, before pouring his coffee, the waitress asked if he was right handed or left handed. When he answered, "Left," she set the mug in front of his left hand and moved his silverware to the other side. Ultimately, it was such a memorable experience for him that, going forward, he measured every other restaurant experience against that.

That's what treating others the way *they* want to be treated looks like. Don't assume. Ask. Observe. Deliver.

---

57   Hal F. Rosenbluth and Diane McFerrin Peters, *The Customer Comes Second* (New York, William Morrow & Co., 1992).

THE OTHER GOLDEN RULE

If you still think the Golden Rule is the better rule, consider this golden rule: *he who has the gold makes the rules*. In other words, whoever has the money, has the power; in this case, it's your customers.

I've never liked the notion that customers have the power. I don't believe customers want to be "in control." That seems like it requires a lot of effort on the part of the customer. Honestly, it's less about control and power and more about expectations and having their expectations known—and met. It's more about brands doing the right thing and doing what's right. It's about customers knocking brands over the head and saying, "We're tired of being treated like crap! Why is this so hard? You ask us for feedback. You capture all this data about us. And yet you still deliver an experience that is primitive at best."

Ultimately, I think a better word for what customers want is a participative role in the relationship. That's not about control; it's about not being one sided or blindsided. Customers have needs and have jobs to be done; companies' products and services help them fulfill those needs or achieve those jobs. Companies are in business to create and to nurture customers. They need each other. So let's shift from control to cocreating.

Just remember, they do have the gold. And they do talk to each other. They share experiences. They are much more informed than they've ever been, and they have higher expectations. They will spend that gold elsewhere if you don't take the time to get to know them and show them that you care about them. That's why this concept of customer-centricity is so important.

He who has the gold makes the rules.

Some of the onus of this rule, though, must be on the customer. With that gold comes some responsibility. It comes at a cost: customers must allow companies to know them. Time to open up, drop the privacy walls/concerns a bit, and let companies in. Let them get to know customers—likes, dislikes, preferences, needs, what customers are trying to achieve, and more.

Of course, customers are only half of the equation. Companies are the other half; they must work with—and adapt to—the customer. How do companies win? Which companies win? Those that win are the ones that:

- are forward thinking and innovative;
- take the time to know and to understand their customers—listen and share insights throughout the organization;
- use predictive capabilities to anticipate—and adapt to—customer needs;
- develop strategies to deliver on those needs;
- use human-centered design (i.e., collaborate and cocreate with customers to design their products and services);
- understand the need for speed of innovation—it's no longer acceptable to take years to develop new products or to upgrade existing ones;
- talk with customers, especially early adopters, to keep themselves ahead of the curve; and
- ensure employees have the tools to do their jobs well and are empowered to do right by customers.

If you choose *this* golden rule, then you must know that all ten of the principles I've outlined in this book must apply. And honestly, it's not that much different from the Platinum Rule. If you understand that he who holds the gold makes the rules, then you know that you need to treat him the way he wants to be treated.

With that, I'm wrapping up the ten principles and moving on to one more chapter about building the business case for customer-centricity. If you want to build a winning organization, you've got to create or show that you can create a customer-centric culture that drives the outcomes you desire. Let's dig into that a bit more.

DO YOU SEE …	WHAT TO DO?	OUTCOMES OR BENEFITS
There is an inherent bias toward treating others the way *you* want to be treated.	Shift your thinking and behavior to understand and then to treat others the way *they* want to be treated.	Better customer experience. Empathy. Advocacy. Loyalty. Growth.
Your marketing department loves to talk about how customers are in control.	Remove "control" from the vocabulary, and replace it with "cocreate." Shift the conversation to focus on building relationships, not dictatorships.	Better customer experience. Empathy. Advocacy. Loyalty. Growth.

CHAPTER 13

Linking Culture to Outcomes

*Measurement is the first step that leads to control
and, eventually, to improvement.*

—H. JAMES HARRINGTON

You've made it this far. You know there's a lot involved in building a winning organization. But is it worth it? Is it worth the time and effort to evolve your culture and your business to be customer-centric?

Yes. Absolutely!

There's data to back up my enthusiasm. Yes, I'm going to hit you over the head with some statistics right now, but it's time to show that this really works, that focusing on culture is good for your employees, your customers, your brand, your employer brand, your business, and your shareholders.

The selling of any concept—and trying to get commitment for anything new in business—is incomplete without linking it to outcomes, not only for the business but also for employees and customers.

I'll make that connection, but first I'll share a few reminders of why the message about customer-centric organizations is so important to get out to leaders today. Unfortunately, when it comes to culture, there's a perception gap. Or it might be lip service. Or it might just be ignorance.

In 2018, PwC conducted research[58] among two thousand respondents in fifty countries on workplace culture. The first shocking statistic was that 80 percent of employees felt that their workplace culture must improve "significantly" or "a fair bit" in order for the business to succeed, grow, and retain the best people. That statistic compares to 51 percent only five years earlier (2013). See, even your employees get it.

The first perception gap statistic PwC uncovered states that 71 percent of C-suite and board respondents believe that culture is a priority on the leadership agenda of their organizations, while only 48 percent of nonmanagement employees agree.

Another perception gap is that 63 percent of C-suite and board respondents believe their cultures are strong ("what we say about culture is consistent with how we act"), while only 41 percent of employees agree.

So employees believe that culture needs to improve but they don't necessarily agree that it's a priority for their leadership team or that it's as strong as their leadership believes it to be. This isn't surprising. There's often a disconnect between what leaders think they're doing or prioritizing and what employees are observing or feeling. Don't be that leader. Don't be so far removed from the day to day and from what's happening within the business that you don't see these things.

Perception is reality.

One final perception gap from this study: employees want a workplace they can be proud of. PwC found that 72 percent of C-suite and board members believe that culture is a strong reason

---

58   "Where Organizational Culture Is Headed," PwC, accessed December 1, 2021, https://www.strategyand.pwc.com/gx/en/insights/global-culture-survey.html

people join their organization. They didn't provide the employee counterpoint, but they did note this gap: 87 percent of C-suite and board respondents are proud of their workplaces, but only 57 percent of employees agree.

You have work to do. These gaps are a problem.

> *For individuals, character is destiny. For*
> *organizations, culture is destiny.*
>
> —TONY HSIEH

In research from 2020,[59] Gallup uncovered that employees working for customer-centric companies are optimistic about their companies, now and into the future.

Among employees who strongly agree that "my organization is the perfect organization for our customers, 37 percent think their company is ahead of the competition; 56 percent are confident in their company's financial future; and 61 percent are convinced that their company is successful and growing."

You have work to do. These gaps are a problem.

Once again, employees get it.

As you probably know, Gallup spends a lot of time on employee engagement and customer engagement work. They found that "fully engaged customers give 23 percent more share of wallet than the average customer." That alone should make you pause and rethink the importance of putting the customer front and center.

---

59   Marco Nink and Jennifer Robison, "Bring Customers into Clear Focus," Gallup, January 6, 2021, https://www.gallup.com/workplace/327524/bring-customers-clear-focus.aspx

Let's get to some real hard data about the connection between your culture and the bottom line. In the past, executives have used the excuse that there's no data on this connection, but they exist.

McKinsey's[60] research points to culture correlating with performance. They looked at more than a thousand companies, and those with cultures in the top quartile of McKinsey's Organizational Health Index had shareholder returns that were not only 60 percent higher than the median companies but also 200 percent higher than companies landing in the bottom quartile.

The values create the value.

—MARC LORE, FOUNDER OF JET.COM

Culture is a driving force in creating value for customers and for the business. Yes, values do create value. First, when your values drive a customer-centric culture, you're putting customers at the center of all you do—again, no discussions, decisions, or designs without thinking about the customer. Solving problems for customers creates value for them—and ultimately creates value for the business. Second, when customers' values align with the brand's values, when customers are aligned with a brand's purpose, they are more likely to prefer, purchase from, and recommend the brand to others than those who are not.

Here's more proof.

John Kotter and James Heskett conducted research years ago, culminating in a 1992 book titled *Corporate Culture and Performance,* and they have continued to build on that research over the years. They discovered that leaders who use culture as a strategic tool (vs. those

---

60   Carolyn Dewar and Reed Doucette, "Culture: 4 Keys to Why It Matters," March 27, 2018, https://www.mckinsey.com/business-functions/organization/our-insights/the-organization-blog/culture-4-keys-to-why-it-matters

who don't) do so quite successfully; these leaders saw the following over an extended period:

- revenue increase fourfold,
- workforces expand eightfold,
- stock prices rise twelve times faster,
- profits climb 750 percent higher, and
- net income grow 700 percent.

In 2019, Grant Thornton LLP and Oxford Economics[61] published a report titled *Return on Culture*. In it, they highlighted several statistics about culture, performance, employee engagement, loyalty, and more. A few noteworthy findings with regard to culture and performance include the following:

- "Public companies with extremely healthy cultures are 2.5 times more likely to report significant stock price increases over the past year.
- "Companies with extremely healthy cultures are 1.5 times more likely to report average revenue growth over 15 percent for the past three years.
- "The average S&P 500 company would see savings of $156M in turnover costs annually if employees were to describe its culture as healthy."

You know the old adage that people don't leave companies, they leave managers. Well, there's an updated—and probably equally, if not more, accurate—version of that, that **people don't leave companies, they leave cultures**. In their research, they also found that respon-

---

61   "Return on Culture: Proving the Connection between Culture and Profit," Oxford Economics, accessed December 1, 2021, https://www.oxfordeconomics.com/recent-releases/return-on-culture-proving-the-connection-between-culture-and-profit

dents with extremely healthy cultures are more likely (45 percent) to retain employees for more than six years versus respondents overall (29 percent). But here's the real proof for the updated adage: half (49 percent) of employees would leave their jobs for a lower-paying job in exchange for a better organizational culture.

The importance of culture is real. It makes a huge difference all around!

LINKING CULTURE TO OUTCOMES

As with any other work you do within your organization, shining the spotlight on culture is also all about the outcomes! Not all outcomes are financial but what I'll call "intermediary outcomes" that ultimately lead to the business outcomes you desire. Let's move to drawing a very clear line from culture to business outcomes, starting with the graphic on the opposite page.

While the graphic may be self-explanatory, let's walk through it briefly.

The foundation of a winning organization is leadership and culture. Leaders must deliberately design the culture they desire, else get the culture they allow. Rather the former than the latter! To do so, leaders must care about their people, and they must create a culture that puts people first. With that foundation—and all of the actions and capabilities I talked about in chapter 5 on employee experience—in place to enable employees to do good work, employees feel a sense of purpose and belonging. They'll feel appreciated and valued, and they'll feel energy and enthusiasm about their work and the workplace.

How are they improving the culture if they're not measuring it?

LINKING EMPLOYEE EXPERIENCE TO OUTCOMES

FOUNDATION

Culture = Values + Behaviors
Leadership Behavior and Actions
Soft Stuff
Hard Stuff

**EMPLOYEE
EXPERIENCE**

Purpose	Valued
Alignment	Appreciated
Belonging	Energy & Enthusiasm
Achievement	

**EMPLOYEE
OUTCOMES**

Engagement	Loyalty (Retention & Advocacy)
Happiness	
Productivity	Creativity
Quality	Innovation

**CUSTOMER
OUTCOMES**

Better Experience
Value Received
Happiness
Satisfaction
Loyalty

**BUSINESS
OUTCOMES**

Employer Branding	Revenue
Recruiting Cycles	Profitability
Competitive Advantage	CLV
Growth	

All of that leads to employee happiness and engagement; to a more creative, innovative, and productive workforce that puts out quality work; and to employee loyalty.

With that as their foundation, employees can deliver an experience for customers that leaves customers feeling valued, helps them to achieve value, solves their problems, and helps them do some job, which culminates in engagement, happiness, and loyalty.

When all of that is aligned, the business benefits include both strong employer and talent branding, shorter and less costly recruiting cycles, increased customer lifetime value, revenue growth, profitability, and a host of competitive advantages that perpetuate all of these outcomes.

If you can't measure it, you can't improve it.

—PETER DRUCKER

MEASURING YOUR PROGRESS

In the aforementioned Grant Thornton research, it was uncovered that 69 percent of companies are not measuring culture, even though 93 percent of executives say they're in tune with their cultures and have worked to strengthen them. How are they improving the culture if they're not measuring it?

There are tools widely available to measure your culture and benchmark your company against others. Just remember, though, that your culture is yours and yours alone. No one can replicate your culture. It's your competitive advantage, so should you really start with benchmarking? No. I get it, though. We all have the need to see where we stand against others. But let's just start by taking a look at our own houses first.

What are some of the ways that you can measure your culture? Here are several factors to look at, some of which I mentioned earlier in the book when I shared findings from research done by Duke University's Fuqua School of Business:

- Employee engagement and turnover
- Leadership actions and behaviors
- Leadership investment in employees
- Leadership and employee alignment to vision, purpose, and values
- People are put before profits, products, and metrics
- Customer insights and understanding inform business decisions
- Values and how they are understood and lived every day
- External communications by the company
- Communications and collaboration within the company
- Alignment of mergers and acquisitions
- Diversity of hires and culture fit
- Employee pride in work and in their employer

In recent years, I've partnered with MarketCulture Strategies, a consulting firm that spent three years talking to customer-centric organizations to identify what they do differently, and I am a licensed user of their assessment tool, as well as a trainer of associated education programs via MarketCulture Academy.

As a result of their research, MarketCulture Strategies developed a customer-obsessed culture assessment, the Market Responsiveness Index (MRI). Through their work, they have proven that a customer-obsessed culture that engages employees to deliver better customer experiences drives profitability. This is a pretty powerful finding.

MEASURING CUSTOMER CULTURE

MarketCulture's research found that eight behavioral practices have a decisive impact on sales growth, profit growth, profitability, customer satisfaction, new product success, and innovation. The table on the opposite page shows how each discipline is a driver of particular business performance outcomes. The check marks indicate validated quantitative relationships between the practices and business performance metrics. Each drives measurable improvements in sales revenue growth, profitability, innovation, customer satisfaction, and new product/service success.

By definition, a company's relative strengths and weaknesses exist only in comparison to those of its competitors. From their research, MarketCulture developed a measurement tool to benchmark a company's customer culture relative to a database of now more than 800 companies and more than 1,500 business units of organizations in the Americas, the United Kingdom, Europe, the Middle East, Africa, and Asia/the Pacific. This measures a business's customer culture capabilities on the eight practices, provides a risk assessment in relation to its strategy, and gives guidelines for action to strengthen the business's customer culture. By taking this reality check, business leaders can assess the ability that the organization has to implement its strategic plan and its customer experience initiatives.

The MRI tool provides benchmarks as percentiles (similar to reported SAT results used by universities for student assessments) rather than raw scores on each of the eight practices. The tool uses a survey assessment completed by all relevant staff in a company or in one or more business units. The result is a snapshot of where the overall company and each business unit stand compared with a large number of other businesses. It measures the behavioral heartbeat of the organization and the degree to which it has a customer culture and can respond to its markets and proactively engage market shifts.

Disciplines	Customer Satisfaction	Innovation	New Product Success	Profit Growth	Profitability	Sales Revenue Growth
Customer Insight	✓	✓	✓			✓
Customer Foresight		✓				
Competitor Insight			✓	✓	✓	✓
Competitor Foresight		✓				
Peripheral Vision		✓				
Empowerment	✓	✓				
Cross-functional Collaboration	✓	✓	✓	✓	✓	✓
Strategic Alignment	✓	✓	✓	✓	✓	✓

197

The MRI scores and qualitative feedback from leaders and employees provide a tangible picture that makes it easy to discuss and identify action priorities. It engages everyone with a unified focus on what to do to strengthen customer culture that improves customer experience and profitability.

NOT ALL CULTURE MEASURES ARE QUANTIFIABLE

Interestingly, not all measures of culture are quantifiable. Some might just be anecdotal. Yup. I know. That squishy part is what scares a lot of people. But honestly, there are quantifiable and not-so-quantifiable benefits and outcomes to everything you do. You've got to look at the complete picture.

To measure a leader, put a tape around his heart, not his head.

—JOHN C. MAXWELL

So let's pause for a moment and consider what a toxic culture looks like, which will give you a better perspective on why a great culture, specifically one that puts people first, is the way to go. You might as well call it a culture of distrust. And oftentimes, it's a situation of "circle the wagons and shoot inward." Here's what that culture looks like.

- There's bipolar behavior. How are employees and leaders going to act today? Will it be the same as yesterday or the polar opposite?
- There's no appreciation or recognition or acknowledgement for a job (well) done.
- Employees no longer collaborate, but they do gossip.

- There seems to be a lack of direction, purpose, mission, and vision—and with all of that comes a lack of clarity.
- Employees are not asked for feedback about the employee experience, the customer experience, or anything else.
- There's infighting among the leadership team.
- Trust is broken. Or nonexistent.
- There's a clear lack of meaningful and transparent communication (i.e., information about the company and how the business is faring from leadership is sparse or nonexistent).
- Accountability is missing, especially among leaders.
- Psychological safety is nonexistent. Fear of recourse rules the day.
- Employees are monitored. Everything they do is tracked to make sure they only do what they're "supposed to be doing."
- Employees are not empowered.
- Leaders operate the business in a siloed manner—and are OK with it.
- Decisions are not based on what's important to the customer but on what leaders think is best for the business.

I've trimmed this list so that it doesn't take up every page of the chapter! But from the list, you can see what I mean when I say that not all benefits are quantifiable. Some of it you just have to experience. And you probably do.

Take a look at what's happening within your company. Do any of these sound familiar? If so, you know that they are productivity killers, inhibit engagement and retention, and drive turnover. But know this: if you feel it, your customers are feeling it too.

Let's wrap up this chapter on a positive note, focusing on a brand we all know puts people first, Costco. In early 2019, their earnings report for the fiscal second quarter, which included the 2018 holiday season, showed 7 percent growth and a 27 percent surge in net income. Comparable store sales and its e-commerce business grew, and employee satisfaction was as high as you'd expect it to be.

Why does Costco see the growth and success that it achieves? It's their people-first culture and approach to business. According to Glassdoor,[62] 82 percent of employees would recommend working at Costco, and 90 percent approve of the CEO. In that same time period, Costco dethroned Amazon[63] when it took over the top spot for customer satisfaction in the American Customer Satisfaction Index for 2018–2019.

Jim Sinegal, cofounder and former CEO of Costco, said in an interview with *Inc.*[64] that "people are happy with a job for more reasons than money. There's generally a pride in the organization. There's an attitude that there's security, that somebody does care about them, that we're offering careers. We're not offering jobs; we're offering careers."

Employee pride in the employer organization pays off huge for customers. And it's a tribute to both the culture and the leadership.

Culture is not the most important thing in the world. It's the only thing.

—JIM SINEGAL

---

62   "Costco Wholesale Reviews," Glassdoor, updated December 1, 2021, https://www.glassdoor.com/Reviews/Costco-Wholesale-Reviews-E2590.htm

63   Jade Scipioni, "Costco Dethrones Amazon as Internet Retail Leader, Report Says," foxbusiness.com, February, 27, 2019, https://www.foxbusiness.com/retail/costco-dethrones-amazon-as-internet-retail-king-report-says

64   Justin Bariso, "In a World Dominated by Amazon, Costco is Thriving," *Inc.*, accessed December 1, 2021, https://www.inc.com/justin-bariso/in-a-world-dominated-by-amazon-costco-is-thriving-they-do-it-by-focusing-on-2-simple-things.html

In an interview with the Motley Fool,[65] Jim stated this when asked about culture and strategy and how they work together:

"Culture is not the most important thing in the world. It's the only thing. It is the thing that drives the business. That's what drives the strategy of our business, is our culture. Recognizing what we stand for in the customer's eyes, and what we mean to all of the stakeholders in our business.

"That is the culture of our business, and we would hope that we'll continue to sustain that. If we do that, if we think in those terms, then I think the strategic planning will come right along with that. We recognize that you've got to continue to be better. Every day when you open the doors, it's like show business. It's another show."

Clearly, it has worked for Costco.

---

65 Brendan Byrnes, "Costco Co-Founder: Culture Is Not the Most Important Thing—It's the Only Thing," The Motley Fool, August 21, 2013, https://www.fool.com/investing/general/2013/08/21/costco-leader-culture-is-not-the-most-important-th.aspx

CONCLUSION

A Letter to CEOs

Most of our obstacles would melt away if, instead of cowering before them, we should make up our minds to walk boldly through them.

—ORISON SWETT MARDEN

This is an open letter to all CEOs to reiterate that designing and living a customer-centric culture means that you're committed to building a winning organization. If you're not a CEO, feel free to share this with your CEO!

Dear CEO:

Have you ever heard the story "What the Hell Is Water?" as told by David Foster Wallace,[66] an American writer? It goes like this:

There are two young fish swimming in the ocean, and they happen to meet an older fish swimming the other way, who says, "Morning, boys. How's the water?" The two young fish swim on for a bit, and eventually one of them looks at the other and says, "What the hell is water?"

This is a great analogy for what must happen with customers in your organization. They must become like the water (i.e., they just are, they are breathed in and out all day long). The customer and

---

66   Jenna Krajeski, "This Is Water," *The New Yorker*, September 19, 2008, https://www.newyorker.com/books/page-turner/this-is-water

her experience are so ingrained in your company's DNA that they just become your new normal: how you do business every day, with the customer at the center of all discussions, decisions, and designs. (It should already be this way, but clearly, it's not.) In this world, customer experience professionals are no longer selling the concepts of customer experience and customer-centricity; they're no longer building the business case and proving the ROI of a customer-centric culture and approach to business. They don't have to. It's just what you do. It's how you do business. It's the air you breathe.

I believe that every company should strive to achieve this level of maturity in their customer-centric cultures, where you look at each other every day and say, "What the hell is customer experience?" Why

No two company cultures are alike. No one can copy your culture.

are we even talking about customer focus or customer-centricity or customer listening or improving the customer experience? It's ridiculous. It should be what every company lives and breathes every day. There should be no concerns over executive commitment or battles to build a business case and prove return on investment. This is a no-brainer.

When customer-thinking is part of your culture, when delivering a great customer experience is ingrained in the DNA, when everyone speaks "customer," then you've achieved the "What the hell is water?" level of customer experience maturity. You'll know when you're there because you'll anxiously await customer insights in your inbox every morning. You will shift how you speak to be in customer language (e.g., instead of "sales process," you say "purchase process"; instead of handoffs, you talk about introductions; etc.), and you'll encourage others to do the same.

While it's on you to deliberately design the company culture to be what it is (or what you allow) and set the tone across the business, it takes every single employee to be committed to it, to work together toward a common goal, to put the customer at the center of all you do. But you must lead them in that direction.

There's a lot of lip service about customer-centricity these days, but until you embrace all ten foundational principles outlined in this book (and listed below) and weave them into the DNA of the organization, well, it's just that—lip service. So let's get you on the path to building a winning organization! Remember the following:

1. Culture is the foundation.
2. Leadership commitment and alignment are critical to success.
3. Employee experience: employees must be put more first.
4. People come before products.
5. People come before profits.
6. People come before metrics.
7. Customer understanding is the cornerstone.
8. Governance bridges organizational gaps.
9. Outside-in thinking and doing, not inside-out thinking and doing.
10. The Platinum Rule rules.

Culture is your thumbprint. No two company cultures are alike. No one can copy your culture. To build a winning organization, you must start with the foundation, your culture—specifically, your customer-centric culture.

In PwC's 2021 Global Culture Survey of 3,200 leaders and employees worldwide, they heard from 67 percent of respondents that culture is more important than strategy or operations. Truly, culture does eat strategy for breakfast. And lunch. And dinner. They also found that 72 percent of leaders felt that their culture helps successful change initiatives happen.[67] All hope is not lost!

I spend a lot of time talking to leaders about the value of a customer-centric culture. It's often disheartening because it seems so obvious; instead, what I see and hear is leaders who:

- still don't make the connection between a great employee experience and a great customer experience.
- focus on growth and acquisition rather than on retention, creating a never-ending vicious cycle (leaky bucket) because they can't keep their customers.
- believe the purpose of the business is to maximize shareholder value. While that may be an outcome, it is not the means or the purpose.
- focus on metrics and metrics alone. Yes, what gets measured gets done. But if you're measuring the wrong thing, you're driving the wrong behavior. And if you're only measuring for the sake of measuring—and not for improving—then you're doing it all wrong.
- need to see the ROI of putting the customer at the center of all they do.
- have no core values or none aligned with customer-centricity.

Here's an uncomfortable—yet indisputable—truth: you are, as Drucker says, in business to create and to nurture customers. Without customers—and especially without employees to create your products and to serve your customers—you have no business. Regardless of company size, region, industry, etc., you are in business for the customer, because of the customer.

---

67   "Global Culture Survey 2021," PwC, accessed December 1, 2021, https://www.pwc.com/gx/en/issues/upskilling/global-culture-survey-2021/global-culture-survey-2021-report.html

I think there are three types of leaders who fill up the "I don't get it" bucket.

1. Those who just simply don't understand that a customer-centric culture drives business success
2. Those who just simply don't care (to understand) that a customer-centric culture is linked to business performance and success
3. And those who think they don't need to focus on employees and customers first because "business is good"

The first two are pretty straightforward, and if you fall into either of those buckets, my hope is that everything you've read in this book has moved you into the "I get it" bucket. As for the third type, let me give you an example because I think a good chunk of you land here.

A friend of mine recently told me how frustrated he is with everything about the company he works for. He shared with me some of the issues. The company is a mess, literally: bad leadership (the entire executive team, including the CEO) that is obviously not aligned, a weak culture, no transparency, no communication, no employee onboarding or training, lots of turnover, no customer onboarding or training, and so much more.

On top of all of that, their customers sign long-term contracts, which means the business has a captive audience. Here's what's crazy: they don't deliver on all of the contract requirements unless the customer complains (imagine that!), at which time the requirement is fulfilled, the box is checked, and the customer is "happy" again. This is no way to do business. It sounds like smoke and mirrors to me. That's an experience, all right—not a very good one.

And yet they are doing well in spite of themselves. Why? Because in their industry, they suck least. First of all, wow. Really? And then, my gosh! What an opportunity they have!

I'm here to tell you that "sucking least" is not a business or a competitive strategy. It's not even an excuse for a business strategy. And it's certainly not an excuse for ignoring the customer. It's lame, and it's lazy. If they really think the business is going "well," they need their heads examined. Imagine what the business would be if they pulled themselves together, did right by their employees and their customers, and became the best in the industry, not just the one that sucked least. Imagine their revenue potential. Imagine what that would force the rest of the industry to do. There are no competitive pressures to do better by or for the customer right now, so the customer suffers. But who cares? The recurring revenue keeps rolling in.

How is that even OK?! It reminds me of playing not to lose versus playing to win. Don't be that company. Don't be that leader. Build a winning organization, one that puts people first and does business ethically.

A customer-centric culture is so powerful. Entire industries have evolved as a result of the customer-centricity of key players. Think about these examples.

- **Hospitality:** Airbnb changed hospitality for good. The industry had pricing, availability, and other issues. Customers love options, and they love staying in a true home away from home.
- **Music:** Apple didn't kill the music industry. The music industry forced customers to buy full-length albums when all they wanted was one song. How many times did you pay ten, twenty, or even thirty dollars for an album back in the day because you wanted that one song you loved?

- **Video:** Netflix didn't kill Blockbuster. Blockbuster did it all on their own. They had ridiculous late fees and really didn't focus on customers' needs and jobs to be done. Netflix just put entertainment at our fingertips, with the click of a button.
- **Retail:** Amazon didn't kill retail. Retailers did it to themselves by not obsessing over customers and by offering poor experiences. Simple, effortless, convenient, personalized shopping rules the day.

While these are all tech brands, technology isn't the reason or the root cause behind the disruption of these industries. Not being customer-centric was the killer. Customer-centric players came in and innovated with and for customers—and won.

I've got news for you, and it's really the bottom line when it comes to business: *it's all about the customer!* It's all for the customer. Everything you do. Everything you create. Every process. Every product or service. Every employee you hire. If you don't infuse the customer into your business and into everything you do, then I don't know why you're in business. It's not to maximize shareholder value. That's an outcome. But the means to get there is to relentlessly focus on the customer, day in and day out. When a great experience with your company becomes the customer's new normal, everyone, including your shareholders, will be happy.

If you need a little reality check, pause for a moment and imagine your business with no customers.

I rest my case.

With love,
Annette

Ideas are commodities. Execution is not.

—MICHAEL DELL, FOUNDER AND
CEO, DELL TECHNOLOGIES

Printed in the USA
CPSIA information can be obtained
at www.ICGtesting.com
JSHW012026140824
68134JS00033B/2899